IMPROVING TRADITIONAL RURAL TECHNOLOGIES

Improving Traditional Rural Technologies

Jeffrey James

Assistant Professor of Economics
Boston University

MACMILLAN

Published with the co-operation of A.T.
International, 1331 H Street, N.W., Washington,
D.C. 2005

First published 1989

Published by
THE MACMILLAN PRESS LTD
Houndmills, Basingstoke, Hampshire RG21 2XS
and London
Companies and representatives
throughout the world

Typesetting by **Footnote Graphics**, Warminster, Wilts

Printed in China

British Library Cataloguing in Publication Data
James, Jeffrey
Improving traditional rural technologies.
1. Technological innovations—Developing
countries   2. Rural development—
Developing countries
I. Title
609'.172'4   T173.8
ISBN 0–333–43711–X

Contents

Acknowledgements

In 1984 Appropriate Technology International of Washington D.C. commissioned a study from me on the subject of upgrading traditional technologies. Two years later they asked me to assist in the design of what they referred to as a replication strategy. The two papers that resulted from these projects were respectively entitled, 'Upgrading Traditional Technologies' and 'The Replicability of Development Projects: a Survey of Methods and Experience'. I am very grateful to ATI for allowing me to include these papers as the main part of my essay.

I am also indebted to Tom Corl, Ton de Wilde, Rob Lichtman, Ted Owens, John Rigby, Howard Pack, Frances Stewart and Judith Tendler for helpful comments at various stages of the research and to Chris Hennin and Charles Weiss of the World Bank for allowing me access to their materials. Ashoka Mody (during 1984), Nasreen Khundker and Prassanan Parthasarathi (during 1986) provided very valuable research assistance.

The author and publishers wish to thank the following who have kindly given permission for the use of copyright material: the Food & Agricultural Organization of the United Nations, for the table from *Agricultural Mechanization in Relation to Production, Employment & Income Distribution in Developing Countries*, Rome, 1981; K. William Easter, for the tables from K. W. Easter and G. Norton, 'Potential Returns from Increased Research for the Land Grant Universities', *Agricultural Economics Research*, 29(4) 1977; The World Bank, for the table from B. Bagadion and F. Korten, 'Developing Irrigator Organizations: a Learning Process Approach' in M. Cernea (ed.), *Putting People First*, 1985; Nancy Birdsall, for the table from 'Population Growth & the Structural Transformation of the Labor Force', Annual Meetings of Population Association of America, Mar. 1985; Robert Chambers, for the table from R. Chambers and B. P. Ghildyal, 'Agricultural Research for Resource-Poor Farmers: the Farmer-First-and-Last Model', Institute of Development Studies, Sussex; Discussion Paper 203, Apr. 1985; Office of the Director-General for Development & International Economic Co-operation, the United Nations, for the table from N. S. Ramaswamy, 'Draft Report on Draught Animal Power as a Source of

Renewable Energy', prepared for UN Conference of New & Renewable Sources of Energy, Rome, 1981; the Free Press, a division of Macmillan, Inc. for Fig. 6.1 from Everett Mr. Rogers, *The Diffusion of Innovations*, 3rd edn, Copyright © 1962, 1971, 1983 by the Free Press; and the *Harvard Business Review*, for an exhibit from John T. O'Meara Jr., 'Selecting Profitable Products' (Jan.–Feb. 1961), Copyright © 1961 by the President & Fellows of Harvard College, all rights reserved.

Boston   JEFFREY JAMES

1 Introduction

It is now more than a decade since the publication of Schumacher's *Small Is Beautiful* (1973). And judging by the subsequent spectacular rise to prominence of the appropriate technology concept in the development literature, one would be entitled to conclude that the central message of this work has been at least thoroughly examined, if not necessarily widely accepted. But a closer inspection of the literature shows that such a conclusion is not at all warranted. For what Schumacher (1973) advocated was a redirection of the development effort in favour of the non-modern sector, and in particular, for a conscious effort to apply an 'intermediate technology' to improving the standard of living of the impoverished inhabitants of this sector.[1] A major portion of the literature, in contrast, has taken as its primary focus the modern sector, and has addressed in great detail, the technological problems that are posed for this sector by international transfers of technology, multinationals, factor price distortions, etc. With few exceptions, the corresponding problems of the non-modern sector have suffered from considerable neglect. Yet, it is this sector that will have to bear the brunt of measures to alleviate poverty in the Third World over the next 30 to 40 years. A principal aim of this volume, accordingly, is to begin to redress this imbalance in the treatment of the subject, and to argue for a renewed interest in Schumacher's original concern with the non-modern sector as the focus of policies for appropriate technology.

Such a perspective has of course, been adopted by the many appropriate technology groups that emerged during the 1970s.[2] These groups have tended to view the solution to the technology problem of the non-modern sector mostly in terms of 'making available' more productive alternatives to the target group living in poverty.

In their work focus has been placed on making available information on technologies which describe the range of known techniques which might be useful to farmers.

Manuals describing different types of tools, and directories of manufacturers of small-scale equipment are examples of this behaviour. Most farmers in developing countries are portrayed by the AT movement as being small, with plenty of labour and little capital. Consequently most emphasis has been given to the dissemination of information about small labour intensive techniques.

Biggs and Clay, 1983, p. 21

Our view is that this approach is incomplete. For one thing, by making what goes on in that part of the non-modern sector in which the poor are located, the exclusive focus of attention, the proponents of this approach are led to an inadequate view of the process by which the benefits of more productive techniques are transmitted to these groups, as well as to a tendency to neglect the dynamic linkages with other parts of the economy on which the degree of ultimate success of policy often crucially hinges. By making the adoption of appropriate technology the end result of the process, this method ignores, moreover, the whole question of the efficiency with which the adopted techniques are used over time. Finally, until very recently,[3] the appropriate technology movement has tended to focus on particular project-level interventions and partly as a result, has neglected the issue of how to replicate these interventions on an expanded scale. Indeed, this problem of replicability has led Marilyn Carr (1985, p. 369) to refer to 'a crisis for the AT movement'. For

although the AT concept gained much support and credibility in the 1970's it stands to lose much of the progress made unless practical proof of its effectiveness can be offered.... Successfully introducing an improved plough, mill, oil-press or water or sanitation system to a few villages, or introducing a new construction or industrial process to a few co-operatives or entrepreneurs is all very well. What is needed, however, is that such products and processes should be adopted, and come into use, in thousands, if not millions, of villages throughout the Third World.

Carr, 1985, p. 369

This volume is concerned to propose a framework that incorporates these neglected aspects of the problem of alleviating poverty through improving the productivity of traditional rural technologies. And on the basis of this extended framework, we review relevant case-study material in order to draw a set of conclusions that will hopefully increase the impact of such efforts in the future. That there is already considerable scope for an enhancement of the impact of appropriate technology is widely acknowledged;[4] over time this objective will become increasingly urgent, as the following section tries to indicate.

THE LIMITS OF A FOCUS ON THE MODERN SECTOR

In a symposium held twenty five years after the publication of his influential dual-economy model, Sir Arthur Lewis posed the question of whether the modern sector 'will grow fast enough to absorb those who wish to leave the traditional sector, in the twentieth century demographic situation' (Lewis, 1979, p. 221). That situation is one in which annual population growth rates of 2 or 3 per cent are extremely high in relation to the historical experience of the European economies, where 'In the second half of the nineteenth century – populations were growing at just over one per cent per annum' (Lewis, 1979, p. 219).

To this considerable difficulty on the supply side, must be added several historically distinctive features on the demand side, that, in combination, make highly doubtful a positive answer to the question posed by Lewis.

First as to the size of the traditional sector. When the industrial revolution began in Western Europe the agricultural population was already down to about 50 per cent of the labour force.... The current LDCs have started with from 70 to 80 per cent in agriculture.... The other side of this is the smallness of the modern sector, which means that even relatively fast growth adds a small number of people....

The second constraint on labour absorption by the modern sector is the transformation of that sector by labour saving devices. In the nineteenth century the expansion of factory employment was paralleled by expansion of shop assistants, clerks, accountants, hotel workers, restaurant workers and so on. All these occupations have been rendered less labour-intensive; office work by the typewriter, the copier and the computer; shop assistants and restaurant workers by self-service; hotel work by cleaning equipment, washing machines and self-service. These innovations have found their way into the LDCs where the effect is to reduce the number of jobs and increase the abundance of labour.

The third difference between then and now is the greater vulnerability of small scale production in the modern sector.... The expansion of small scale activity in the modern sector is an important part of the development process.... Particularly remarkable is the degree of market integration between large and small firms, with the large sub-contracting to the small for intermediate parts and services. Much has been written about this in the context of Japan, but there is plenty of it in any modern industrial economy. There seems, however, to be less of it currently in LDCs than one would expect.

Lewis, 1979, pp. 221–3

One way to assess these historically distinctive conditions is to estimate the length of time that is likely to elapse before the absolute size of the non-modern sector begins to fall (that is, before the economy reaches its 'turning point'). For this purpose, several authors have made use of an identity which expresses the rate of change in the labour force in the non-modern sector in terms of this sector's initial share in the labour force and the rates of change in the total labour force and in the modern sector's labour force.[5] The most recent of the estimates to be prepared on this basis is by Birdsall (1985). Though she is concerned with agriculture versus non-agriculture, rather than with the modern and traditional sectors, her results (shown in Table 1.1) amply convey the problem of delayed structural transformation facing most contemporary developing countries.

Table 1.1 shows, for different projected rates of population growth ('standard' or 'rapid') and growth of the labour force in the non-agricultural sector at 2 or 4 per cent per annum, the year when the turning point occurs and the absolute numbers in the agricultural sector (relative to 1980 as the base year) at that time. For example, assuming 'rapid' population growth and non-agricultural employment growth of 4 per cent per annum, the turning point in Kenya will occur in the year 2040, at which time the numbers in the agricultural sector will be almost 5 times as great as they were in 1980.

Although a few developing countries – South Korea and Brazil – have already reached their turning points, for many others the transition is only likely to occur in 30 to 40 years time. By then, moreover, the absolute size of the agricultural sector will have swelled substantially. 'In Bangladesh, for example, assuming a 4 per cent annual growth of employment outside agriculture, there is likely to be under the standard population projection a two- to three-fold increase in the number of people working in agriculture in the next four decades' (Birdsall, 1985, p. 23). The most extreme outcome, however, is projected for Kenya. 'Assuming the standard projection

Table 1.1   *Growth of agricultural labour force under various assumptions*
(index 1980 = 100)

Country	Non-agricultural employment growth at 4% a year		Non-agricultural employment growth at 2% a year	
	Standard	*Rapid*	*Standard*	*Rapid*
Kenya (78% of labor force in agriculture, 1980)				
Index	947	475	1380	660
Turning point[a]	2045	2040	2065	2045
Thailand (76%, 1980)				
Index	158	151	230	207
Turning point	2010	2005	2025	2025
Bangladesh (74%, 1980)				
Index	263	188	. . .	301
Turning point	2030	2010	2060+	2040
India (69%, 1980)				
Index	136	135	228	206
Turning point	2005	2005	2030	2025
Malaysia (50%, 1980)				
Index	111	113	231	205
Turning point	2000	2000	2015	2015
Egypt (50%, 1980)				
Index	102	104	244	198
Turning point	2000	2000	2025	2020
Brazil (47%, 1980)				
Index	112	n.a.	n.a.	n.a.
Turning point	1970	n.a.	n.a.	n.a.
Korea (66%, 1960)				
Index	109	n.a.	n.a.	n.a.
Turning point	1960	n.a.	n.a.	n.a.

[a]*Notes*: The year when the agricultural labor force starts to decline.
n.a.   Not applicable.
. . .   Not available.

Source: Birdsall (1985, table 6).

of population increase is correct, the labour force in agriculture will
be more than nine times its present size (947 per cent) before it begins
declining in 2045' (Birdsall, 1985, p. 24).

THE RELIANCE ON TRADITIONAL RURAL TECHNOLOGIES

The scenarios for Kenya, Bangladesh and India contained in Table
1.1 are alarming in part because they mean that so many more people

are likely to become reliant on traditional (and usually unproductive) agricultural technologies. By the term traditional we shall refer to any technology that has been in use for a relatively long period of time, such as 25 years. And from our definition of technology we shall exclude all the biological and chemical aspects of production that have been discussed in the literature dealing with the Green Revolution. On the other hand, we shall want to include in our definition, consumption, as well as production technologies. The current extent of reliance on traditional agricultural technologies defined in this way is suggested (albeit very crudely) by the data in Tables 1.2 and 1.3. The former groups rural farm technologies into three broad types, namely, those operated by hand, those which rely on draught animal power and those relying on mechanization in the form of tractors. The table also shows the shares of these three forms of technology in the developing as well as the developed world in 1975.

Table 1.2   *Area cultivated (million ha) in 1975*

| | Total | | Power sources | | | | | |
| | | | Hand labour | | DAP | | Tractors | |
	Area	%	Area	%	Area	%	Area	%
Developing countries	470	100	125	26	250	52	104	22
Developed countries	644	100	44	7	63	11	537	82
World	1 123	100	169	15	313	28	641	57

The above excludes China. China cultivates 100 million ha, 50% of which is cultivated by DAP and 50% by tractors. Contribution of hand labour and percentage shares are not known.

Source: Ramaswamy (1981, p. 21).

Table 1.2 confirms what one would expect – that the reliance on non-mechanical forms of technology is substantially greater in the poor than in the rich countries. And, within the former, as Table 1.3 indicates, much the same systematic variation appears to hold between regions according to their levels of income.

This tendency for the shares of the two non-mechanical forms of rural farm technology to be positively associated with the 'stage of development' appears to offer some basis of a workable concept of 'traditional technology.' But to what extent would it be valid if one were to rigidly identify these two categories with the term traditional, as it was defined above? In many parts of the world, a close identification would in fact seem to be easily justified. Take first the

Table 1.3   *Percentage share of different power sources in total power input in the agriculture of 90 developing countries: 1980*

Region	Labour	Draft animals	Machines
90 developing countries	66	29	5
Africa	81	16	3
Far East	64	34	2
Latin America	56	25	19
Near East	63	25	12
Low income countries	63	35	2

Source: Ahmed and Kinsey (1984, Table 1.2).

situation in Africa, about which a UNIDO study has noted that, 'In many cases . . . Africa's small farmers – numbering over 300 million if women and children are included – . . . are using virtually the same kind of hoes, knives, scythes, and animal-drawn ploughs as were depicted in Egyptian monuments of 5000 years ago' (UNIDO, 1983, p. 130). Much the same description can be applied to many countries of Asia. In India and West Pakistan, for example, 'the bulk of farmers utilize a comparatively limited number of implements most of which have remained unchanged for centuries, (Johnston and Kilby, 1975, p. 359). Or again, in relation to draught-animal power in India (which has the largest supply of this type of power in the world), one commentator has observed that, 'the bullock-cart and carts drawn by other animals have undergone little change in design over the past several decades. There has been no systematic effort . . . to transmit the benefits of modern science and technology to the bullock-cart, rural transportation and the communication system as a whole,' (Ramaswamy, 1979, p. 48).

To the extent then that one can, for the above reasons, closely equate non-mechanical with traditional technologies, it is evident that for much of the developing world these technologies dominate the land areas devoted to rural farm production. The same conclusion may be restated in terms of labour, if it is (reasonably) assumed that mechanical technologies are operated on the basis of wage labour and that hand and animal-powered methods are conducted on the basis of non-wage modes of production. Then, by subtracting the wage-labour share from the total agricultural labour force, one arrives at an estimate of the proportion of the latter that is dependent upon traditional technologies. In 1970, this proportion amounted to some 70 per cent for the developing countries as a group;[6] a figure that is similar to the share of non-mechanical technologies given in Table 1.2.

These estimates exclude rural non-farm employment, which comprises an average of roughly 25 per cent of the rural labour force in those countries for which data are available.[7] It is of course impossible to classify this activity as traditional on the same basis (i.e. source of power) as for the farm sector. All that can be said is that since much non-farm activity is small-scale and of low productivity,[8] there is a presumption that most of the technology with which this activity is associated has remained substantially unaltered over a relatively long period of time.

THREE FRAMES OF REFERENCE IN THE IMPROVEMENT OF TRADITIONAL RURAL TECHNOLOGIES

Taken together, the two preceeding sections suggest that historically unprecedented numbers may become reliant on traditional rural technologies before the turning point is reached in many of the poorest countries. And it is perhaps especially true of these countries that the private sector cannot be relied upon to provide an adequate response to the problem.

One reason is the lack (or poor enforcement) of a patent system, which tends to undermine the commercial incentive to make improvements to traditional technologies because there are few other means by which an innovator can appropriate the gains to such innovations. In the case of simple farm equipment, for example, 'New innovations which demonstrate ready market acceptance and which are easily fabricated are quickly emulated by others. Unless the design is complex, uses unusual materials or methods in its fabrication or has a tightly circumscribed market, there is little an innovator can do to protect the design from being copied or to capture or restrict the benefits from its use' (Duff, 1985, p. 4).

Even in the absence of this appropriability problem, however, there may be severe supply-side constraints that render unlikely a repetition in the East African context of the historical experience of the United States. That experience was distinguished in particular by

the critical role played by local blacksmiths, tinkerers and inventors working closely with innovative farmers. Frequently, it has been a local farmer who has defined "the problem" and has turned to a local workshop to translate an idea into a new or modified piece of equipment in a process that often involves much trial and error. However, the rudimentary development of local manufacturing capabilities in East Africa and the limited experience of farmers with mechanical equipment means that *exclusive reliance on that sort of private R&D would be an unacceptably slow process.*

Johnston, 1984, p. 49, emphasis added

For this reason, Johnston concludes that 'there appears to be a need for a more purposive effort by publicly supported R&D activities' (Johnston, 1984, p. 49).

In general, the efforts that are required to improve traditional rural technologies may be based, as Table 1.4 indicates, on three alternative frames of reference.

Table 1.4   *Alternative frames of reference in the improvement of traditional rural techniques*

Method	Associated frame of reference	Retention of traditional techniques
Upgrading	'Bottom-up'	Significant
Descaling	'Embodied modern technology'	None
Replacement investment	Existing scientific knowledge	None

Upgrading is an approach that may usefully be characterized as operating from the 'bottom-up'. For in a very general sense, its distinguishing feature is the implication that there are intrinsically worthwhile elements of the traditional technology (such as accumulated knowledge, cultural values, skills, designs, etc.) which need to be retained in the process of creating an improved alternative. There are, in contrast, two other approaches with which are associated quite different assumptions as to the appropriate frame of reference, and what characterizes both these approaches (as Table 1.4 indicates) is a rejection of the need for retention of significant elements of the technologies whose productivity is to be increased.

The descaling strategy has as its frame of reference the technology shelf that has been built up over time, and which, for the most part, comprises technologies developed in and for the rich countries. It is by the 'scaling-down' of these existing technologies to the village level, that advocates of this approach seek to raise the productivity of producers who, formerly, were reliant on traditional methods.

The third approach (that of replacement investment) takes neither traditional nor modern technology as its point of departure. Instead, the existing base of scientific and technical knowledge is applied directly to generating an alternative technology, which, as in the case of descaling, *replaces* rather than builds upon the elements of traditional technologies. (It is, of course, often difficult to meaningfully distinguish between upgrading and replacement of traditional technologies, since it is unlikely that the latter approach will incorporate *none* of the elements that comprise such technologies and the distinction, consequently, becomes one of degree. The same arbitrariness applies with respect to the comparison between descaling and replacement investment.)

(a) Upgrading

As noted above, upgrading is based on the observation that there are elements of the traditional technology which are of value in the creation of an improved alternative. Frequently, however, these worthwhile elements seem to go unobserved by the formal R&D system. One reason is that

> Junior field extension staff, ... being low in the government service, have a vested interest in exaggerating differences between themselves and local people; and the distinction between 'superior' scientific and 'inferior' indigenous knowledge protects and legitimates their status... There are also likely to be problems among more senior staff engaged in R&D. Established professional values dictate that rewards should be given to those who make original contributions to knowledge, achieve breakthroughs at the level of theory, and publish their finding in internationally reputable journals; but offer relatively little incentive to individuals to go out on a limb with approaches involving ITK [indigenous technical knowledge].
>
> Howes and Chambers, 1980, p. 332

A World Bank review of water supply and sanitation technology in the Third World illustrates the tendency referred to in the quotation with particular clarity. The authors of the review found that

> the differences in climate, socioeconomic conditions, and the sheer

scale of the problem make it difficult to apply technical data from an industrial country directly to conditions in a developing country, even when the data are of a 'scientific' nature. This is particularly true with respect to nonconventional waste-disposal technologies. The influence of conventional Western research in wastewater collection and treatment on attitudes in most developing countries cannot be overestimated. *Wastewater research, even when it is going on in a developing country, in many cases follows Western models and turns its back on local traditions and practices.*

Rybczynski *et al.*, 1982, p. 45, emphasis added

More specifically,

as sewerage has become synonymous with sanitation, it has been assumed that improved sanitation implies drastic change. It is probably for this reason that so little literature has been identified dealing with indigenous excreta disposal practices – it has been assumed that these are of little importance as they will eventually be replaced by sewerage. As a result, the potential for upgrading existing practices has been largely ignored.

Rybczynski *et al.*, 1982, p. 38.

To the extent that examples such as these characterize the formal R&D system, the potential afforded by an upgrading approach tends to be undervalued accordingly. What is ignored, in particular, is the potential that derives from the close adaptation over time of traditional technologies to the natural and engineered local environment. For when incorporated in a more productive alternative, these elements of traditional technologies have significant *instrumental value* in promoting its adoption, maintenance and efficient usage. This general point is well illustrated in the specific case of an upgraded traditional pit latrine. The new version (the ventilated improved pit latrine) embodies almost all the features of the traditional version, but in addition, it relies on a vent pipe to control the major disadvantages of the latter. Among the reasons for the reliance on the traditional technology as the basis upon which to generate the new latrine were the following.

In rural areas it is best to design the latrine as far as possible in the same way as the local houses are constructed, so that self-help construction and maintenance can be used with only the minimum of external instruction and supervision. Such an approach is not only likely to be the least cost one, but it also ensures that the latrines blend in well with their environment, such aesthetic consideration may well prove to be one of the more important factors affecting local acceptance and sustained use of latrines in rural areas.

Morgan and Mara, 1982, pp. 24–5

It is considerations such as these that led the survey on water supply and sanitation technologies quoted above, to conclude that, 'Any attempt to upgrade or improve the existing situation, and this is surely the only strategy that has any chance of success, will have to be based on sound understanding of existing resources, limitations, and possibilities' (Rybczynski *et al.*, 1982, p. 45).

Similar arguments have been adduced for other types of traditional rural technologies. Water mills in Nepal, for example, are said to have numerous specific advantages deriving directly from their close integration into the local environment. 'The people are able to make these mills in their own surroundings. Wood and stones are the materials mainly used. A few iron parts are added. . . . As people can use materials from their rural surroundings the cost is almost nil. . . . Repairs are no real difficulty' (Bachmann and Nakarmi, 1983, p. 15).

It would be a mistake, however, to confine the relevance of this essential point to only the 'hardware' aspects of traditional rural technologies. One needs to pay attention, as well, to traditional craft skills as well as to traditional forms of organizing production, especially in the case of 'public goods' such as irrigation and sanitation. With respect to irrigation, for example, Coward points to the existence of a large number of locally constructed and operated systems around the world.

Within this set of experiences are a large number of 'silent successes': traditional, usually small-scale systems, many of which have operated for decades and centuries. . . . These traditional irrigation systems offer important insights regarding the solution of organisational problems, particularly at the level of the terminal unit; not that they can simply be duplicated in other situations but that they suggest important principles of organisation which can be applied in other specific settings.

Coward, 1977, p. 224

(b) Descaling

Descaling takes as its frame of reference modern technologies whose evolution has usually been accompanied by a rise in the scale of production. As such, the most obvious problem with this approach is the sheer *extent* of the descaling that will normally be required to render the technology operational at the village level of traditional technology.

In some cases (where 'technical rigidities'[9] are not too severe) this problem may be greatly lessened by the use of earlier (and hence smaller-scale) versions of modern technologies. Examples here include the partial oxidation method in gas generation used in small nitrogenous fertilizer plants and the vertical-shaft kiln used to produce cement.[10] Many of these earlier vintages, however, are associated with products that are produced to lower standards of tolerance (partly because these earlier methods permit the use of lower quality inputs).[11] This association, in turn, may undermine the competitive viability of the descaled alternatives in certain circumstances but it need not invariably do so. In China, for example, this problem seems to have been avoided partly because the products of descaled technologies are used for different purposes than those that are produced by more modern technological vintages. As Perkins has put it:

> the existing quality of the output of these [descaled] plants is adequate for their intended use in the rural areas. For example, poor quality cement is suitable for dams with earthwork cores; unstable chemical fertilizer is made usable by mixing it with green manure in the compost heap.
>
> Perkins *et al.*, 1977, p. 113

If one way to strengthen the potential for descaling is through *earlier* vintages of modern technologies, another approach may be to make use of some of the *newly emerging* technologies. For some aspects of these (most notably the miniaturization associated with microelectronics), appear substantially to facilitate this process.[12] For example,

> In the past, and in the absence of an alternative, normal practice has been to scale down conventional large hydro machinery, including the hydraulic governor. But this has proved to be both an

uneconomic and an unmanageable approach. Defective mechanical or hydraulic governors have been the main cause of failure in these small hydroelectric plants. They are too complex to maintain at the village level in developing countries.

Recognising this, a hydro engineer and an electronics engineer ... designed a low cost electronic device to fit into micro-hydroelectric schemes ... in order to control the electrical output from the alternator (that is, controlling the 'load' rather than the 'flow') ... It has been widely accepted as a major step forward in making micro hydroelectric plants viable for small rural communities.

Bhalla *et al.*, 1984, p. 122

There are, finally, various institutional factors that tend to facilitate descaling efforts. One of them is the existence of rental markets which enable small-scale producers to gain access to descaled technologies without actually having to own them. In countries such as the Philippines these markets are extremely well-developed, as evidenced by the fact that 'harvesting and threshing equipment, tractors, and motor vehicles, are used on about five to seven times as many farms as those who own them' (Binswanger, 1982, p. 16). A second facilitating factor is the organization of production on a co-operative rather than a village entrepreneurial basis. In the descaling of crystal sugar in India, for example, an attempt was made to organize production on these lines.[13]

In general, then, the potential for descaling is dependent not only on technical/engineering factors but also on institutional variables, whose behaviour will vary substantially from one situation to another.

(c) Replacement Investment

As noted above, the valuable instrumental elements of traditional technologies derive from the closeness of their adaptation over time to the environment. But because this environment may itself change – sometimes suddenly and dramatically – replacement investment, rather than upgrading, will tend to be the appropriate approach to the problem. A good example is to be found in the circumstances that gave rise to the replacement of the water wheel by mechanized irrigation in the Saga Plain Area of Japan. From the middle of the

18th century until the 1920s the water wheel, operated by human labour, was the technology used in this area to raise water. But beginning around 1900, 'The equilibrium of the technology was shattered ... by events happening outside the agricultural sector' (Francks, 1979, p. 532). In particular, rapid industrial expansion resulted in a marked fall in the agricultural labour force and a consequent substantial increase in wage rates. Because there were limits to the extent to which the water wheel could be adapted to the changed economic circumstances, it soon became clear that 'the introduction of a mechanized pump to replace the water wheel was essential to further progress in agriculture'

(Francks, 1979, p. 532).

A SCHEMATIC OUTLINE OF THE VOLUME

A schematic outline of the volume is shown in Figure. 1.1.

The previous section dealt with the alternative frames of reference in the improvement of traditional technologies (that is with the first of the relationships shown in Figure 1.1). Chapter 2 is concerned with the second relationship, namely, that between the diffusion of improved technologies and the rate of their adoption within the scope of a particular project. This link, as noted earlier, is the focus of many of the appropriate technology institutions (though some of them pay primary attention to the technical or engineering problems of improving traditional technologies). It was also suggested previously that this focus fails to adequately describe the nature of the economic relationships that link the adoption of improved technology to the supposed beneficiaries among the poor. This neglected issue is the subject of Chapter 3. The major argument of this chapter is that even if adoption is widespread among the target group, the immediate and future impact of this on poverty is a highly complex matter, the underlying variables in which are entirely neglected in the very assumptions that are usually made in the appropriate technology approach. Chapter 4 takes up another central issue that this approach has tended to neglect, namely, that of seeking the replication on a large scale of projects that prove successful at the micro level (this is the fourth and last of the relationships shown in Figure 1.1). The final chapter considers the major implications for policy of the findings for each of the linkages shown in the figure.

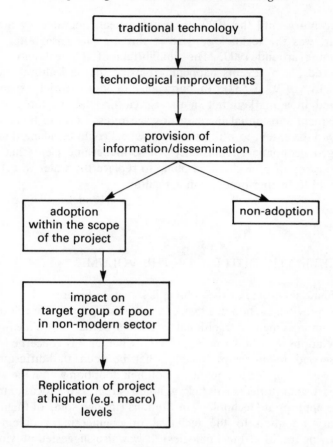

Figure 1.1 A schematic outline of the volume

2 Diffusion and Adoption: the Lessons of Experience

This chapter comprises an analysis of project case-study material, with the aim of isolating the main factors that seem to account for the cases of success as well as of failure in the diffusion and adoption of improved rural technologies. The focus is on upgraded versions of traditional technologies, though a few cases fall into one or other of the alternative categories (namely, downscaling and replacement investment) described in Chapter 1. Even with this somewhat limited focus, however, the data set does not purport to be inclusive of all relevant experience. Rather, it should be viewed as the outcome of a brief, but intensive survey of the English-language literature conducted mostly during 1984.

One of the principal conclusions that emerges from a study of this material is that, though there are some general lessons to be drawn, the choice of a suitable approach to diffusion *needs to reflect the variation in the nature of the technology that is upgraded*. There are, in particular, three distinctions that need to be made, namely, between: (a) technologies for production and those for consumption, (b) technologies that can be diffused on an individualistic basis as opposed to those that require some communal form of organization, and (c) technologies that are located 'on the farm' in rural areas and those that are associated with non-farm activities. Taken together, these distinctions enable us to draw up a typology of cases, in the form of the matrix shown in Table 2.1 (some of the cases which we shall analyse are contained in the matrix for illustrative purposes).

Each of the cases shown in the six cells in the matrix is defined by a

Table 2.1   *A typology of cases*

	Individual	*Communal*
Consumption	Wood-stoves, rain collectors	Sanitation, water supply
Production		
Farm	Tools, animal carts	Pumps
Non-Farm	Food-processing, crafts (e.g. pottery)	Crafts (e.g. communal kilns)

a suitable method of diffusion, we ought thus to be able to offer a set of guidelines for the successful diffusion of any *particular* type of technological improvement (representing a particular *combination* of characteristics).

FARM VERSUS NON-FARM PRODUCTION TECHNOLOGIES

One of the most significant features of peasant farming in many countries is the presence of a marked seasonal shortage of labour.[1] This feature of the farming system has a crucial bearing on the question of whose productivity needs to be raised if upgrading is to result in the kind of expansion of farm output that will promote widespread adoption of the new technology (expressed formally, the concern here is with the appropriateness of the bias in factor-saving). For unless the improvement in traditional technology makes some contribution to reducing the peak labour requirements (by raising the productivity of this input and therefore, effectively increasing its supply), it is unlikely to meet the needs of the farm sector, however much it may raise the productivity of other inputs. The converse of this proposition is that the ease with which innovations can be disseminated may be substantially increased if they are expressly designed to reduce the seasonal labour bottleneck. The experience of the ILO/UNDP Tanzania project on appropriate agricultural implements clearly illustrates this important point.

In seeking to define the characteristics of a set of improved farm implements that would be widely acceptable to the villagers, those concerned with the project came to the conclusion that this required 'careful attention to the constraints under which farmers live, because such constraints determine the limits of what is feasible. The project ... was developed within the limits of such constraints, and it is from this initial awareness that its success resulted'.[2] One of the most important of these constraints was a seasonal shortage of labour for weeding which the new technique, because of its reduced labour requirements, was able to break. And even though this method did not represent a substantial reduction in total costs compared to the traditional technique, it was nevertheless 'a gain of great significance to the farmer'.

A second major feature of farming systems which warrants special consideration is the marked variation in environmental conditions between and often within regions, a degree of variation that may be described (see ch. 4) in terms of a high index of environmental sensitivity. What this sensitivity implies for the requirements of a successful upgrading effort, is that improved technologies need to be designed (or adapted) in a manner that is closely reflective of the features of a particular geographical area. For instance,

> An outstanding feature of Taiwanese agriculture implements is the degree to which each tool has been designed for its special task and specific environment. An example is the harrow, one of the eight types of tools used in secondary tillage. There were nine kinds of harrows reported in 1952. . . . Since 1952 the animal-drawn tyned tiller and the disk harrow have been introduced. A single one of these harrows, the standard knife tooth, has twelve regional variants. Width, length, material and number of teeth, shape of tooth blade, and method of affixing teeth are adapted according to local typography, field size, soil structure and available construction materials.
>
> Johnston and Kilby, 1975, p. 357

If adaptations to specific environmental circumstances were a major feature of the successful Taiwanese case, the failure to effect these types of adaptations is said to have been an important reason for the disappointing experience of the Chilalo Agricultural Development Unit (CADU) in Ethiopia. Initiated under the Third Five Year Plan (1968–74), CADU was given the task (among other things) of conducting 'adaptive research in the major ecological zones of Chilalo'. Included in this research programme was to be the design of ox-drawn plows, harrows and carts, and other improved farm implements.

> But acceptance of the prototypes by small farmers to date has been very disappointing with the exception of the ox-drawn harrow. One reason for the rather slow acceptance of most of the improved farm tools seems to be that *sufficient consideration was not given to environmental variations between localities* and farmers' preferences as to, for example, the shape and weight of certain tools. For example, the ox-drawn plow was rejected by many farmers primarily because they found it too heavy to be carried on their shoulders from their homes to the farm, and too heavy to be pulled by their oxen.
>
> Tecle, 1975, pp. 11–12, emphasis added

The two features of peasant farming systems that were described above, are not peculiar to this component of the rural sector; they apply in varying degrees also to certain non-farm activities. Traditional open pan sugar technology, for example, is said to suffer from a pronounced labour shortage during the crushing season[3] and many non-farm activities are characterized by a degree of environmental sensitivity, which, though not as high as is usual in the farm sector, is still of a magnitude that is uncommon by the standards of the urban sector. But what mainly distinguishes rural non-farm activities from those that take place on the farm are the *dimensions* of the upgrading process.

Firstly, the upgrading process in the non-farm sector has to pay particular attention to *skills*, since it is the level of these (especially in crafts production) that is a major determinant of earnings in the sector.[4]

Secondly, whereas farms produce mostly undifferentiated products, the output of the non-farm sector is often significantly differentiated from competing goods, and this fact has a major bearing on what is required for successful upgrading. It means, in particular, that in addition to the production technology, the product itself may often need to be upgraded, a dual requirement that is attested to by several case studies.

Early efforts to upgrade the village pottery industry in India, for example, were confronted with the problem that the traditional product, a non-porous red-coloured variety made from local clays, had lost ground over time to whiteware articles made from China clay. As a result, upgrading the village potters' technology on the basis of the former proved to be inadequate. 'The only alternative which appeared to stand a good chance of success was to initiate the manufacturing of whiteware at the village potters' level' (Garg, 1976, p. 176).

Upgrading of traditional products need not, however, require such a major alteration; what may be required instead, is a reduction in the *variation* in the quality of a *given* product. Any attempt to replace cement with a village-produced alternative, such as lime-pozzolana, for example, will have to confront the problems that

> Unfamiliarity of the product will initially make users suspicious of it, and unwilling to make the risk of using it in preference to the well-known and reliable existing product. The fact that it is made in the village with less quality control than can be expected in a

factory, and not subject to any recognised standard or specification, will increase the lack of confidence. . . . Any sub-standard
material which finds its way on to the market particularly in the
early stages of production when users are unfamiliar with the
product, will increase the potential users' lack of confidence in the
material.

Spence, 1978, p. 59

Much the same problem appears to have had a lot to do with the
failure of the attempt by the Khadi and Village Industries Commis-
sion (KVIC) in India to upgrade the technology of the cottage match
industry. Lack of uniformity in the quality of the matches associated
with this project made it difficult to market the goods through the
existing network of wholesalers and retailers, even though these
agents were offered margins that were higher than conventional
rates. And when the KVIC 'lost the hold over the market function –
the crucial rein – all other development measures failed to push the
programme to success' (Moulik and Purushotham, 1983, p. 126).

Up to this point, we have stressed the essential differences in the
required form of the diffusion process between the farm and rural
non-farm sectors. But the case-study evidence indicates that there are
also numerous *common* requirements in the two sectors. The most
important of these common dimensions of appropriateness in the
design of improved technologies are listed below.

(a) Costs

In relation to the farm sector, we took note earlier that, if they are to
be widely disseminated, new technologies will often need to break
the production bottleneck that is imposed by the seasonal shortage of
labour. Though there are in principle many forms of new technology
that are capable of meeting this requirement, it is generally only
those that can do so at a sufficiently low cost in relation to farm
incomes that will be spread successfully. In the case of traditional
producers in the poorest developing countries, this requirement
places highly stringent limits on the capital costs of improved
technologies. And to meet these, all available means of reducing
costs have normally to be employed.

In Taiwan the importance of this point had been grasped even by
the early 1950s, as the following description of the period clearly
reveals.

Farm implements in Taiwan are comparatively cheap and this is due to the farmers' low purchasing power. Manufacturers often have to sacrifice quality in order to maintain a low price. If sturdy and highly efficient farm implements were to be made, their prices will have to be raised; farmers because of their financial stringency, will not be able to buy these implements even if they are aware of their good performance. In other words, the farmers in Taiwan should be temporarily satisfied with the minimum serviceability of implements available.[5]

Exactly how cheap most of these implements were, can be gauged from the fact that the average price of half of the total stock in existence in 1952 (i.e. 160 items) was less than US$5 at 1970 prices (and the majority of animal drawn implements fell in the US$10–40 range).[6]

The same type of concern with methods of cost reduction as a key determinant of widespread dissemination has recently been expressed in the advocacy of 'village technology'. This concept, which arose out of the ILO/UNDP Tanzania project mentioned above, is meant to describe a technology that 'takes the fullest possible account of the cash constraint on subsistence farmers, while at the same time permitting great reductions in labour input per unit of output, as well as lightening much of the physical arduousness of agricultural work – no mean consideration for the malnourished' (Macpherson and Jackson, 1975, p. 116). Those concerned with the project sought to distinguish this concept from 'intermediate technologies' (such as cultivators, harrows, etc.) that are manufactured mainly from metal and which, partly on this account, are often beyond the means of subsistence farmers. Village technologies, in contrast, are made chiefly from wood and other cheap local materials and are shown to represent, on average, a savings in cost of some 60 per cent over the intermediate alternatives.

The difficulty, of course, lies in creating pressures/incentives/ attitudes that are favourable to the concerted and creative efforts to reduce the costs of improved technologies that have been described above. In the Taiwanese case, these propitious circumstances were provided on the demand side by gradually rising cash sales per farm unit together with a high degree of competition between a very large number of producers, and, on the supply side, by the absence of significant economies of scale in the production of farm tools.[7] In the Tanzania project, the favourable outcome arose mainly from a close

interaction between the officials involved and the villagers for whom
the new technologies were designed. Frequently, however, neither
economic circumstances nor the attitudes/behaviour of researchers
are conducive to achieving the level of costs that produce widespread
dissemination.

In the upgrading of traditional Indian ox carts, for example, a
contrasting set of economic circumstances from those that obtained in
Taiwan led to a very different outcome. Among the deficiencies of
these carts are rough and loose bearings and iron-rimmed tyres on
wooden or iron wheels that lead to low carrying and earnings
capacity, damage to animals and to roads.[8] An improved vehicle,
introduced by Dunlop, has a steel axle, steel wheels, roller bearings
and pneumatic tyres. But this vehicle, though it is considerably more
efficient than the traditional cart, has had only a very limited impact
on traditional producers. One reason for this is said to be its relatively
high cost – approximately double that of the traditional alternative.
And the reason for the inappropriately high costs (relative to the
incomes of traditional producers) has been stated as follows.

> Because of the low volume of tyres required, tyre companies have
> no incentive to manufacture specifically designed tyres for ADVs
> [animal drawn vehicles]. The same points hold good for ball
> bearing or taper roller bearings. Now ADVs are using truck
> bearings which are costly as they are meant for high speed, high
> precision, heavy loads, etc. ADVs need slow speed and cheap
> bearings.
>
> Ramaswamy, 1979, p. 62

On occasion, the cost of improved technologies fails to match the
resources available to traditional producers, even when they are
designed specifically for this group. Consider, for example, what
occurred when the Central Tasar Research and Training Institute in
Ranchi, India, operating under the aegis of the Central Silk Board,
attempted to effect an improvement in the traditional method of
cooking cocoons. For this purpose, a new cooking chamber was
designed which allowed a faster and more efficient process. But the
new cooker, at a cost of 300 rupees, proved too expensive to be
widely adopted by the target group of low-income households.[9]

(b) Scale

The costs and scale of technologies are often closely related, so that innovations which are excessively costly in relation to the resources of target groups among the poor tend also to be of too large a scale. Thus, intermediate technologies in the Tanzanian example referred to above, are mostly both more expensive and of larger size than the village technologies and in the case of the cocoon-cooking equipment in India, the scale, as well as the cost, was inappropriate to the objective of securing widespread adoption of the new equipment among the poor.

But the appropriateness of the costs and scale of upgraded technologies has to be defined not merely in relation to the size of holding (in the farm sector) or the unit of production (in the non-farm sector), but also *to the institutional capability of organizing the ownership or use of these technologies on a communal basis*. In the case of the improved cocoon-cooking equipment, this capacity was apparently absent, for the technology demanded a change in the 'method and organization of production apart from market arrangements which could not be possible with the target beneficiaries' (Moulik and Purushotham, 1983, p. 308). In other cases, however, the required capability does exist, and this substantially alters the definition of the appropriate scale (and costs) of production.

One example is the upgrading of traditional pottery technology in India, that was referred to earlier in another context. In some of the locations in which the production of whiteware was organized, the firing of the pottery was carried out in a centralized workshop that had been established by the local government, but other components of the process were performed at the level of the village potters' own workshops. It was only after the initially satisfactory experience with this form of organizing production, during which the potters had acquired experience in producing whiteware, that they were encouraged to build kilns in their own workshops. Taken together, these and other efforts to upgrade the traditional technology created additional employment for some 10 000 people in Uttar Pradesh, an experience that led M. K. Garg to observe that 'the most critical factor [in scaling-up village technology] is the type of organisational set-up required to initiate, expand and support such a programme for at least a dozen years or so' (Garg, 1976, p. 177).

The Japanese experience is an especially noteworthy illustration of how the appropriate scale for upgrading (and replacement investment) can be separated from the individual unit by various forms of co-operative arrangements. After the First World War in that country,

There were many kinds of farm machines whose prices were too high for individual households to be able to buy and for which the minimum required scale of operation was too large for individual farm households to be able to use them efficiently. Therefore, there was scope for a minor cooperative to perform the function of the agent for the joint investment of these individual farm households.

Ishikawa, 1981 p. 327–8

Indeed, Ishikawa has demonstrated that, in the 1930s, the proportion of listed farm machines that were jointly owned was between 10 and 25 per cent of the total ownership.

One needs to be extremely cautious, however, in drawing policy conclusions from the successful Japanese experience with co-operatives. For this experience was very largely the product of an organizational capacity among the rural population that had been inherited from the feudal period. And as Hayami (1975, p. 207) has pointed out, in this respect, 'The conditions of agricultural development surrounding the countries in South and Southeast Asia today are certainly very different from those prevailing in Japan at the Meiji Restoration.' But one needs also to stress the policy aspects of the Japanese experience, and in particular the attention that was paid to the need for technological adaptations and innovations.

(c) Simplicity

In addition to being appropriate with respect to cost and scale, many of the instances of widely diffused improvements to traditional technologies are characterized by simple manufacture, maintenance and repair requirements in relation to levels of available skills. Table 2.2 shows a number of such illustrative cases (including two consumption technologies, in the area of sanitation).

CONSUMPTION VERSUS PRODUCTION TECHNOLOGIES

The second main distinction on which our typology is based, is between consumption and production technologies (though in some cases, of course, elements of both types may be involved, as when, for example, rain collectors are used to store water for domestic needs and also for watering livestock).

The importance of the distinction here, turns, principally on the

Table 2.2   *The dimensions of appropriateness*

	Cost	Scale	Simplicity
ILO/UNDP improved farm implements in Tanzania	60% lower than intermediate technology	village level	'enables the villagers to construct and keep in working order a whole variety of agricultural equipment'
Water pump in Saga Plain, Japan	Capital cost of installation per hectare of land equal to annual wages of one hired worker	village co-operative level	'easy to operate and fitted into the existing layout of water channels'
Handpump in Bangladesh	700 takas in 1979	Individually owned and operated	'easy to install and maintain and the necessary skills are available locally'
Ventilated improved pit latrines in Zimbabwe	often the least-cost technically feasible sanitation 'technology' in rural areas	Family or village community level	'since the architectural style of these latrines is essentially the same as that of their houses, the householders have the necessary skills to do regular maintenance work'
PRAI improved latrine in India	'Within the financial means of the villager'	Village household level	'can be made locally, and the skills required for manufacturing the parts, erecting the latrine and operating it can be easily acquired by the villagers'

Sources:
For Tanzania, Macpherson and Jackson (1975, p. 104).
For Japan, Francks (1979, p. 536).
For Bangladesh, Howes (n.d., p. 5).
For Zimbabwe, Morgan and Mara (1982, p. 21).
For India, Garg (1976, p. 180).

fact that whereas production technologies relate to the producing unit (be it a farm or non-farm activity), consumption technologies are normally used in *the household*. And within this unit, the key person involved is often rural women.[10] The consequences of this fact for the dissemination of improved wood-burning stoves, an important example of upgrading a consumption technology, have been described by Agarwal as follows.

> The status of women within the household could be a significant factor in wood-stove adoption, especially where adoption requires cash expenditure, by virtue of the fact that although women are the potential users of the innovation, and therefore in the best position to assess its advantages and disadvantages, it is men who usually handle the household cash and make decisions on how it is spent.... Where men make the decisions, the purchase of an improved stove may not get priority, especially where the only advantage perceived is greater leisure or convenience in cooking for the women. This is also one significant reason why attempts to promote wood-stoves in the same way as watches and radios (whose primary users and main beneficiaries in the rural areas are men) are likely to be ineffective.... Likewise, the status of women within the community enters as an influencing factor in a number of significant ways ... rural women usually have no direct access to institutional credit or to independently disposable cash income to purchase new innovations/technologies; and they seldom have access to information on new innovations. Also, there is a strong ideological bias in extension services which is likely to work against the direct involvement of, or consultation with, village women in the experimental designing of wood-stoves for their use – an involvement which the Guatemala and Ghana case studies indicated as being a significant feature in effective diffusion.
>
> Agarwal, 1983, p. 370

What distinguishes the dissemination of this, and other similar types of consumption technologies (such as for water supply and health-care), is therefore the extent to which the process is embedded in, and hindered by, a complex set of social relationships. And, as Agarwal points out, the more inhibiting are these relationships, the less appropriate is a 'top-down' approach to dissemination, i.e. one in which problems of diffusion are basically viewed as problems of information/communication and persuasion. Instead, it is the nature of the social relationships themselves that more urgently need to be altered. Where this has, in isolated cases, proved possible, the results have been encouraging. The Jamkhed rural health project in Maharashtra illustrates the possibilities.[11]

Initiated by two doctors in 1970, it sought to train and use local women in the delivery of curative and preventive health care. And although

> the majority of these women are illiterate, they are quick to learn, and their ability to communicate with and gain the confidence of the other village women (helped by commonality of diction, tradition and values) has been one of the strengths of the programme. There is a conscious attempt to overcome caste barriers ... and to maintain a relationship of equality betwen the professionals and the non-professionals.
>
> Agarwal, 1983, p. 371

The success of the project can be gauged from the fact that its operation has spread from an initial 8 villages to a current figure of over 70.

In another, similar example, the Dian Desa organization was able to introduce and successfully disseminate rain-water collectors made of bamboo and cement, to a village in Indonesia.[12] One of the most interesting aspects of this project, and indeed the work of Dian Desa in general, is that its point of departure represents an inversion of the 'top-down' approach. That is, 'Traditional communities' perceptions, values, ways of thinking, natural resources, etc. are first determined before any innovations are pursued. And this process's point of entry is local technologies that at least reflect local perceptions.' (Soedjarwo, 1981, p. 2).

In the context of the bamboo-cement rain-water collectors, the design of the new technology originated directly from three elements of traditional practice, namely, the plaiting of bamboo, the catching of rain water and the local availability of bamboo. And in the dissemination of the rain-water collectors, involvement of the local community was again actively sought. First, 'Dian Desa started a "dialogue" with 20 local people and together made a decision to build some bamboo-cement rain-water collectors. . . . Before building more collectors, a village seminar was held. In this seminar/meeting each person who received and used a rain-water collector explained about its advantages and disadvantages.' (Soedjarwo, 1981, p. 7) What appears to have been especially important to the villagers was that 'they were pleased and proud about being able to build the rain-water collectors themselves.'

INDIVIDUAL VERSUS COMMUNAL LEVELS OF ADOPTION

Our third and final variable is concerned with the implications of the *level* at which adoption decisions are taken in the use of different types of technologies. In particular, we shall consider the implications for the dissemination process of decisions that are taken at the level of the community, rather than the household or individual.

According to some authors, the importance of this distinction has to do solely with the question of group consensus, and the difficulty of achieving this in the case of a large and heterogeneous group of inviduals. Jéquier (1976, p. 52), for example, makes this point in the following way.

> The purchase of a transistor radio, a sewing machine or a tin roof for instance is a decision which is taken by the individual or his family on the basis of his own resources and ability to pay.... When it comes to something like a village water distribution system, a sewage system or a new type of crop, the decision to innovate is no longer in the hands of the individual, however directly he may be involved. Decisions of this type require some form of consensus which is much more difficult to achieve than consensus in the family.

Various techniques for overcoming this problem in decision-making for small communities have been proposed.[13] However, these techniques are as yet neither well-known nor widely used.

While there is, of course, no question that the difficulties of obtaining consensus are inimical to the adoption of new technologies at the communal level, it does not follow that *perfect consensus* will always achieve this result. The reason – indeed, the more fundamental problem of group action – is that when the group is large, no single individual has any incentive to join a communal scheme. For by definition, he cannot make a perceptible contribution to the group scheme, and since no one in the scheme will react if he fails to contribute, there is no economic incentive for him to do so.[14] And the resulting inherent tendency for the large group to fail to act in accordance with its common interests applies not merely to decisions regarding the adoption of new technologies, but also to their operation and maintenance once installed. (It is, in fact, often mainly for this reason that poor maintenance is one of the most frequently encountered problems of providing communal facilities, such as improved sanitation technologies).[15]

The case-study evidence suggests two ways in which this intrinsic difficulty of group action may be lessened. The first is to use social pressure as a substitute for the above-mentioned absence of an economic incentive. In this way, the economic gain from leaving the burden of securing the benefits of communal technology to others can be offset by the loss in social status that would result from such unco-operative individual action. A very good example of how social pressure can be made to serve the common interests of the community is to be found in the introduction of a new sanitation technology into the village of Yalcuc in Mexico.

The decision to install the latrines in this village, comprising forty-three households, 'was made within the context of a community project; all the aura of the leadership and the pressures of social control were brought to bear on the villagers. Gradually, all the men in the community signed an agreement in a village meeting signifying their commitment to the collective decision to install latrines (Elmendorf and Buckles, 1980, p. 19). Equally significant, is the observation by two students of the dissemination of the new technology, that, 'The costs (in money and time) of installing a latrine were perceived by many as minor compared to the costs (in social pressure, loss of good will, and deterioration of solidarity) of *not* installing one (Elmendorf and Buckles, 1980, p. 20).

It should be apparent from this example, that for the effective use of social pressure a relatively small group is needed, one in which the members can have direct contact with one another. In a larger group, the members do not know each other and it is accordingly more difficult to exercise social pressure on individuals who fail to contribute to the objectives of the group. From this observation it follows (and this is a second lesson from the case-studies) that, insofar as it is possible to maintain a relatively small group as the relevant organizational unit, the problem of group inaction may be considerably ameliorated. Nowhere is this lesson more evident than in the experience of irrigation technology.

A common feature of traditional irrigation systems is that they are small in size; these small systems, moreover, are invariably further divided into smaller sub-units.[16] This sub-division into mini-units can be interpreted in terms of the discussion above as an attempt to overcome the problems of co-ordination, conflict and co-operation that are inherent in the operation of an irrigation system. In relation to Laos, for example, one observer has noted that the small size of the irrigation association is rooted in the elements of village sociology. In particular,

Lao society is founded on reciprocal solidarity bonds connecting the members of a group; *in order for these bonds to function satisfactorily the group must not have more than 70 or 80 members.*

Coward, 1977, p. 228, (emphasis added)

More generally, Coward has suggested that

Small groups (especially if differences of social status and social class are relatively minor) are able to employ special mechanisms of reciprocity to achieve relative order and conformity. While this can also be achieved with large-scale organizations such as bureaucracies, these organizational arrangements are often dependent upon technologies and infrastructures (for example, roads and telephones to facilitate mobility and communication) not available in developing countries.

Coward, 1977, p. 228

It does not seem unreasonable, therefore, to propose that maximum use of these indigeneous, small-scale units should be made in attempts to upgrade traditional irrigation systems. Otherwise, the advantages of cohesiveness that are associated with these small groups will be lost and the new system will tend towards inefficiency. This is precisely what occurred, for example, in Java and Bali, as described by Ishikawa (1981). He points out (p. 338) that the traditional patterns of organisation in these regions (based on strong village communal ties), 'worked well for developing, operating and maintaining local irrigation systems'. Recently, however, the size of the organisational unit for these systems has apparently become significantly greater, and at the same time, the extent of government involvement has increased considerably. The result, according to Ishikawa, has been that 'The autonomy and responsibility of the traditional irrigation groups have been correspondingly reduced. Side by side with this, a number of inefficiencies have arisen relating to construction and water management' (Ishikawa, 1981, p. 338).

However, as Coward points out, there may be a solution to this dilemma. Large-scale, modern irrigation systems may be designed in a manner that combines the technical and economic requirements of large size with elements of traditional social systems. The Chinese 'melons-on-a-vine' design illustrates this approach. It uses a main canal system to supply a series of small reservoirs or ponds, which, in turn serve a smaller command area. 'Thus, while part of a larger system, each pond group has some independence of action regarding water allocation' (Coward, 1977, p. 231).

SOME GENERAL LESSONS

In the previous section, we tried to show how the characteristics of (traditional) technologies give rise to differences in the way that innovations should be promoted; differences that, in our view, were shown to fully justify a typologically sensitive approach to the problem. But at the same time, there is a need to recognize any lessons that are *common* to the cases referred to above.

One such lesson is that an appropriately upgraded technology (that is capable of widespread dissemination) should be viewed as a multi-dimensional concept, although, as suggested above, the dimensions of appropriateness and their relative importance will vary with the characteristics of each type of technology (products, for example, will be a highly relevant dimension in the dissemination of some technologies, but not in others). But whatever these dimensions of appropriateness happen to be, it is the ability to determine and satisfy the user requirements with which they are associated that is crucial to the outcome of policies for diffusion. Indeed, it is what may be termed the criterion of 'user needs understood' that best discriminates between the cases that appeared to be successful, and those that may be designated as failures, regardless of whether the technologies involved were for production (farm or non-farm) or consumption, individuals or communities. Table 2.3 provides some support for this general conclusion by showing the role attributed to this factor (by the relevant authors) in the outcome of selected case-studies, drawn from those considered above, and representing each dimension of the typology matrix (in Table 2.1).

If understanding user needs does (on this very limited evidence) seem to be a crucial variable determining success or failure in the dissemination of innovations, a high degree of local involvement at the design stage is invariably the only means by which this can be achieved. The generation and dissemination of improved technology, that is to say, ought to be seen as closely related, rather than as entirely distinct stages of a sequential process. From a policy point of view, however, a focus on local involvement still leaves one with the problem of how such involvement is to be achieved.

According to Coombs and Ahmed (1974) the problem has to be tackled through policies for training additional researchers and for bringing about a basic change in their attitudes to the dissemination process. Thus,

Table 2.3   *The role of 'user needs understood'*

Case	Outcome	Author's observations
ILO/UNDP improved farm implements project in Tanzania (MacPherson and Jackson, 1975, p.118)	Successful	'The project was devised within the limits of such constraints [under which farmers live], and it is from this initial awareness that its success resulted'
Wood-stoves – a summary of case experience (Agarwal, 1983, p. 372)	Mixed	'The familiarity of the stove designer with the cultural milieu of the community where the stoves are to be promoted, and the adaptation of the stoves to suit specific users' needs, is a crucial factor in adoption'
Rain-water collector (Indonesia) (Soedjarwo, 1981, p. 18)	Successful	'Understanding a community's perception takes a lot of time. Though physically the result of this process has not yet been seen, the utilization of this process itself has to be worth as much as other activities.... Using the community's participation to fuse the community's perception into the development process gives much better results than the 'top down' process'
Water supply and sanitation technologies – review of LDC experience (Rybczynski *et al.*, 1982, p. 37; Kalbermatten *et al.*, 1980, p. vii; Elmendorf and Buckles, 1980, p. 27)	Generally unfavourable	'It is becoming accepted that the optimal solution and often the only possible solution, is the one that takes into account local and circumstantial resources.... The amount of interaction with the eventual users must be greatly increased.... The diffusion of the new technologies and their acceptance is related to the involvement of the communities in the planning as well as implementation of the projects'
Improved farm implements in Ethiopia (Tecle, 1975, p. 53)	Failure	'Distribution of improved farm implements to farmers was not possible because the prototypes developed by CADU were found to be unacceptable to farmers'

Table 2.3   *The role of 'user needs understood'* (continued)

Case	Outcome	Author's observations
Irrigation pumps, Saga Plain, Japan (Francks, 1979, pp. 532 and 535)	Successful	'Selection of appropriate characteristics in areas such as scale, mobility and complexity was the crucial element making for a successful choice. . . . it involved particularly close contact between farmers and officials for reasons which were, in part, peculiar to the environment of the Saga Plain'
Improved technologies for rural industry in India – a review of the evidence (Moulik and Purushotham, 1983, p. 344)	In most cases a failure	'it became difficult for the functionaries . . . at the implementation level to perceive the real technological needs of the users'
Improved farm implements in Taiwan (Johnston, 1981, p. 33)	Successful	'Dispersed manufacture of such equipment facilitates feedback between farmers and manufacturers and thereby helps to insure that the implements that are produced are adapted to the needs of the local farming systems'
Farm equipment innovations in Southern Africa (Ahmed and Kinsey, 1984, p. 318)	Failure	'Despite years of R&D in institutions scattered over the region, the small and medium-sized farmers of eastern Africa have yet to experience any real benefits in terms of improved equipment suitable to their farming circumstances'

it should be standard practice (though it rarely is now) for researchers to leave their laboratories for frequent visits with sample farmers in their own fields, to listen to the farmers' questions and hypotheses, to observe production problems and results under normal (nonlaboratory) conditions, to take the farmers into their confidence – in short, to become direct parties to the extension and feedback process. *For this to happen on a sufficient scale however, there must be many more well-trained researchers and a new attitude on their part toward contact with farmers.*

Coombs and Ahmed, 1974, p. 123 (emphasis added)

In part, attitude reform would seem to be a question of altering the narrow, single-disciplinary focus that is characteristic of most research activities in agriculture. Many observers now recognize that 'the usual approach which has concentrated on the development and testing of equipment by agricultural engineers is simply not effective' (Johnston, 1981, p. 39).

A reform of attitudes will often also have to be sought in the restructuring of the system of incentives and other aspects of the way in which research is organized. In India, for example, institutes that were set up explicitly to upgrade traditional rural non-farm technologies are organized as mere extensions of the central government administration, and as such, have assumed many of the same attitudes and rigidities that are inimical to a close and effective relationship with the target groups. More specifically, a 1983 study has drawn attention to the fact that the rules according to which research is initiated and approved, credit is granted for the diffusion of innovations, and promotion of staff is given, all seem to be highly unsuitable for the flexible and imaginative type of operation that the generation and dissemination of new technologies in the rural areas often require.[17]

The direction of these various attitudinal reforms is similar to that which proponents of 'farming systems research'[18] and 'farmer-first-and-last' models[19] regard as necessary for understanding the user needs of small resource-poor farmers. And as Table 2.4 indicates (specifically in relation to the 'farmer-first-and-last' model), this is a direction that contrasts sharply with the methodology of the dominant 'top-down' or 'transfer of technology' approach, in which 'Highly trained civil, mechanical and agricultural engineers, medical scientists, agronomists and others develop technologies in laboratories, workshops and experiment stations and then attempt to transfer them to would-be clients' (Chambers and Ghildyal, 1985, p. 3).

If fundamental changes in location and learning are evidently required by the 'farmer-first-and-last' model, it also seems clear that these changes (especially when they are carried out on a wide scale) will tend to be resisted by scientists and others (such as extension agents and large farmers) whose interests are generally better served

Table 2.4   *Contrasts in learning and location*

	Transfer of technology	Farmer-first-and-last
Research priorities and conduct determined mainly by	Needs, problems, perceptions and environment of scientists	Needs, problems, perceptions and environment of farmers
Crucial learning is that of	farmers from scientists	scientists from farmers
Role of farmer	'beneficiary'	client and professional colleague
Role of scientist	generator of technology	consultant and collaborator
Main R&D location	experiment station, laboratory, green house	farmers' fields and conditions
Physical features of R&D mainly determined by	scientists' needs and preferences, including statistics and experimental design	farmers' needs and preferences
	research station resources	farm-level resources
Non-adoption of innovations explained by	failure of farmer to learn from scientist	failure of scientist to learn from farmer
Evaluation	farm-level constraints	research station constraints
	by publications	by adoption
	by scientists' peers	by farmers

Source: Chambers and Ghildyal (1985) p. 21.

by the 'transfer of technology' model.[20] For this reason alone, one might anticipate formidable obstacles in the implementation of the former approach. And one might accordingly expect to find a literature that had addressed itself to these predictable difficulties.

Yet, according to Heinemann and Biggs (1985, p. 62),

because the FSR [Farming Systems Research] literature has not focussed on theoretical issues of implementation and institutionalisation to any great extent, 'the method' has been considered in

isolation, under abstract ideal conditions; and the absolute importance of institutional issues has been overlooked in the formulation
of the FSR programme proposals. Instead there has been a
tendency for policy analyses to take place in ____ ____ a vacuum
where administration and implementation issues are seen as
"minor details" to be left to bureaucrats or project staff. Indeed, it
is only after the programme has been initiated that the full
significance of these issues is recognised. And because they were
not considered in the initial analysis, they are dismissed as
unfortunate external effects that prevent 'the method' from func-
tioning efficiently, i.e. they become 'problems'.

Heinemann and Biggs argue in favour of an alternative approach
which would

internalise the administrative and institutional issues of programme
implementation and give them consideration from the outset.
Programme proposals would explicitly recognise the institutional
characteristics and capabilities likely to be encountered, and
suggestions would be based upon an analysis of these issues.

Heinemann and Biggs, 1985, p. 62

An interesting example of the type of research that would seem to
be called for by this more realistic approach, is Simon Maxwell's
study of the difficulties that arise in the introduction of social
scientists to agricultural research programmes, especially in the
context of farming systems research. He shows that these problems
are likely to comprise far more than just the 'usual difficulties of
interdisciplinary cooperation and group dynamics' (Maxwell, 1984,
p. 46). There is, in addition, the fact that the very appointment of a
social scientist *implies* the need for basic structural change in the
organization of a research system. What is required, in particular, is a
transition from an organizational model in which autonomous
specialist departments are managed by a head officer (the so-called
'role culture' model) to one that is job or project oriented (a 'task
culture'). Because any such restructuring is 'In an obvious sense ... a
struggle for power' (Maxwell, 1984, p. 40), it contains also a clear
political component. Maxwell concludes that these organizational
and political issues should be 'recognised as inherent to the process of
introducing multidisciplinary research and should be accommodated
in planning for such research' (Maxwell, 1984, p. 46).

CONCLUSIONS

There are several characteristics of traditional technologies that give rise to differences in the way that new technologies should be promoted. Among the most important of these typological differences were thought to be between technologies for production and those for consumption, between those that can be disseminated on an individualistic basis as opposed to those requiring some communal form of organization and, finally, between those that are located on the farm and those that are associated with non-farm activities. One of the clearest lessons of the chapter, however, is that whatever the combination of these characteristics that any particular technology comprises, it is the ability to determine the user requirements with which they are associated, that primarily determines the success or failure of policies for dissemination. What is much less clear, on the other hand, is how the close involvement of users at the design stage that this condition demands, is to be achieved in environments where relationships between the relevant groups are, from this standpoint, highly unfavourable. So far, the proponents of farming systems research seem to have paid insufficient attention to overcoming these and other institutional difficulties.

3 The Impact of Adoption on the Poor

If adoption of improved technology was all that mattered to improving the welfare of the poor – as tends to be posited in the appropriate technology approach – there would be no need to proceed beyond the lessons of the case-study material that was reviewed in Chapter 2. However, as was pointed out in Chapter 1, the immediate and future impact of adoption on poverty is an extremely complex matter, depending as it does on a set of variables that are normally neglected in the implicit assumptions of the appropriate technology approach. Some of the most important and restrictive of these assumptions have to do with its characterization of the nature of poverty in the non-modern sector.

THE IMPLICIT CHARACTERIZATION OF POVERTY IN THE NON-MODERN SECTOR

In the appropriate technology approach, the poor in the non-modern sector tend to be viewed as a relatively homogeneous category (in terms of the mode of production and occupational groups) that is related to technology only through the process of production (i.e. through the incomes that this process generates). The economic impact of technical change on poverty is consequently viewed in the narrow terms of how the increased incomes that are thereby generated accrue to the homogeneous category of poor households. In reality, however, the poor are not only highly heterogeneous in terms of their relationship to technology through the production system, but they are also affected by technology in their capacity as consumers (Table 3.1 contrasts this view of the poor with that implied by the appropriate technology approach.) Recognition of these factors demands a quite different view of how technical change in the non-modern sector may impinge on patterns of poverty in this sector.

Let us consider first the production side of the question, and specifically, the issue of how heterogeneous groups among the rural poor, namely, the owners of productive assets, the unemployed, and "the working poor," might be differentially affected by the improvement of traditional technology. It is at this point that one has to confront the crucial question, thus far ignored, of exactly *whose* productivity is to be raised.

Table 3.1 *Alternative characterizations of the relationship of the poor to technology*

	System of Production	Consumption
Appropriate technology approach	Homogeneous	Ignored
Realistic approach	Heterogeneous	Important

The input (capital, labour or land) whose productivity is increased will initially face a decline in demand because the existing level of output can then be produced with less of this input. However, because the rise in productivity is also a decline in costs, output will often tend to expand to a degree that more than offsets this decline in the demand for the input to produce each *unit* of output. The *net* impact on demand for the input will then be positive. If then the supply increases sufficiently, the price of the input will remain fixed; at the other extreme is the case in which there is no forthcoming increase in supply, and the entire change in demand is reflected in the increased *price* of the input (Figure A3.1 in the appendix to this chapter sets out these relationships more formally).

The general point is that the direct effect of technical change on the prices and quantities employed of the various inputs depends on the degree to which it is biased in favour of raising the productivity of one input rather than another, the extent to which output increases in response (which factors together determine the change in the demand for the input), and the change in the input supply that follows the alteration in the demand. And, to complicate matters further, one needs also to take into account the mode of production – whether it is based on a wage or non-wage family system – which will determine the manner in which the gains from given increases in the productivity of inputs are distributed (see Figure A3.2 in the appendix for an elaboration of this last distinction). The outcome of all these relationships, in turn, will determine, as shown in Table 3.2, the direct impact of technical change on the heterogeneous groups comprising the poor. The last column and row of the table are intended to capture the fact that much traditional activity is organized along pre-capitalist (e.g. family) lines and that this activity cannot properly be classified according to the other divisions in the table that are based on capitalist relations. In particular, people working according to the pre-capitalist forms of organization cannot be termed 'employed' in the relevant sense, nor can their earnings be classified into the categories of profits and wages.

Table 3.2   *The direct impact of technical change*

	Unemployed	Working poor	Owners of productive assets	Precapitalist organization of production
Fall in wages	X	−	X or −	X
Rise in wages	X	+	X or −	X
Rise in employment	+ or X[a]	X	X	X
Fall in employment	X	−	X	X
Rise in profits	X	X	+	X
Rise in earnings	X	X	X	+

+ = gain from change
X = position unchanged
− = lose from change

[a]*Note*: This depends, of course, on whether or not the unemployed (underemployed) are willing to accept new wage-employment opportunities.

What Table 3.2 shows is not merely that a particular form of technical change may leave the situation of certain poverty groups unchanged, but that it may even cause a *deterioration* in their economic welfare. An increase in wages, for example, may be harmful to the interests of those who own productive assets. An increase in labour productivity will lead to unemployment, unless the associated expansion in output is proportionately at least as great. This, in turn, depends heavily on the price elasticity of demand. The more inelastic is this demand, the more limited will be the output (and hence employment) expansion associated with technical change. In this connection, it is important to distinguish between foodgrains which have a highly inelastic demand and many of the products of rural industry which have a much more elastic demand. Specifically, whereas the price elasticity of demand for maize and wheat in developing countries is frequently not more than 0.3, the products of rural industry (such as processed sugar, pottery, soap, cement, etc.)

are characterized by a relatively *elastic* demand (i.e. greater than 1).[1] Sometimes, of course, the inelasticity of demand for foodgrains may be alleviated by export markets, but in general, labour-saving technical change in the production of these commodities (as occurs, for example, in post-harvesting operations) is especially likely to result in unemployment.[2] And if it does, the possibility of further losses for those in poverty is raised by interactions between some of the changes shown in Table 3.2 (i.e. the rows). In particular, technical change which increases the numbers of unemployed may often also produce a decline in real wages[3] (and conversely for changes which lead to an increase in employment).

The economic effects described in the previous paragraph are of a direct kind; in addition, one needs to take account of any indirect effects of technical change on the poor. With respect to employment, for example, the direct effect refers to the impact of technical change in only the sector where the change occurs. Indirect employment effects, in contrast, arise from various interdependencies *between* sectors (which economists refer to as 'general equilibrium' effects). For instance, technical change in a given sector increases per capita income (the 'income effect') and also tends to decrease the price of the good (the 'price effect'). If the income effect exceeds the price effect, output (and hence employment) of the sector which did not experience technical change will increase, despite the relative rise in the price of the goods that it produces.[4] In many cases the sum of these and other indirect effects offsets (albeit sometimes only partially) the direct employment losses from labour-saving technical change. This is said to be the case, for example, with the introduction of portable threshers in the Philippines.[5] As shown in Table 3.3, these machines would generate considerably less direct employment (equal to a loss of 22 per cent) compared to the use of manual methods of producing an equivalent increment of rice. On the other hand, mechanization appears to have the effect of increasing employment outside the agricultural sector. 'Domestically produced threshers would generate employment in the manufacturing sector. Increased rice output would have a positive effect on employment via consumption linkages' (Duff, 1985, p. 17). From the point of view of the poor, however, the problem is not only that the employment losses occur in the sector where these groups tend to be concentrated, but that in addition the losses turn out to be large in relation to the gains.

The differential effects (direct and indirect) of technical change on poverty that were described above, derive particular importance in

Table 3.3 *Employment implications of a 1% increase in rice production using manual or mechanical threshing methods, Philippines*

Method	Agricultural sector (direct increase)	Indirect increase (Non-agricultural sectors)	Total increase
	thousand man years		
Manual threshing	15.9	27.1	43
Portable thresher	12.4	27.6	40
% difference	22	2	7

Source: Duff (1985, table 7).

relation to the fact that the proportions of the different groups in poverty vary substantially from one country to another (as Table 3.4 shows). It means that a particular form of technological improvement will have a different distributional impact depending on where it is applied. For example, the introduction of mechanized threshing in the Philippines led (as noted in Table 3.3 above) to an overall saving of labour compared to the manual method of production. And the labourers that were displaced by this new technology came predominantly from the category of landless labourers, one of the poorest groups in the country.[6] In Thailand, in contrast, where a category of landless labourers scarcely exists, the same new technology had no such pronounced inegalitarian effects. Such labour as was displaced

Table 3.4 *Occupational composition of the poor (percentages)*

	Employer	Self-employed	Employee	Housewife	Unemployed
Malaysia, 1970 (poorest 49%)	0.5	51.8	41.8	2.3	3.6

	Employer	Self-employed	Employee, private sector	Employee, public sector	Sharecropper
Brazil, 1960 (poorest 31%)	0.5	51.0	37.0	3.0	8.0

	Employer	Self-employed	Salary earner	Worker	
Chile, 1968 (poorest 46%)	0.0	24.0	5.0	71.0	

	Employer	Self-employed	Employee	Unemployed	Other
Trinidad and Tobago,* 1975/6 (poorest 42%)	0.4	15.1	25.6	18.6	40.3

Note: The table on which these figures are based classifies households by monthly income and occupation of head of household.

Source: Griffin and James (1981) p. 26.

by mechanization came instead from households which benefited from the increased efficiency of mechanized threshing.

In general, if improved technology is to have a significantly favourable impact on poverty in a particular country, it will need to be well matched to the specific composition of the poor in that country. Referring to Table 3.4, it is clear, for example, that technical change will do little to solve the poverty problem in Trinidad and Tobago, unless it is associated with a significant increase in employment.[7] Similarly, unless the working poor in Chile are able to share in the productivity gains from improved technologies, the result will be only a slight impact on poverty. To this extent, technical changes which *appear* to fall into the category of being appropriate, may not in fact have a significantly greater impact on poverty than those which are more obviously inappropriate because they *entirely* bypass the groups represented by the columns of Table 3.3, and instead distribute increases in employment, wages and profits solely to members of the richest groups such as labour 'aristocracies' and owners of large firms.

If, therefore, it is important to take into account the differential impact of technical change on the heterogeneous occupational groups comprising the poor in each particular case, it is also necessary to consider the *disaggregation* of these categories in order to allow for the impact on particular groups (e.g. women) *within* them. What occurred as a result of the introduction of improved reeling technology in the Indian tasar silk industry demonstrates the importance of heterogeneity within (as well as *between*) the groups living in poverty. In particular, the improved technology appears to have generated

The significance of this altered structure for poverty derives in part from the fact that

> a definite structural change in the employment relationship in the industry. Most certain, is the decline of silk reeling activity by the women folk and giving the place to a small number of machine employed hands.
>
> Moulik and Purushotham, 1983, p. 274

Among low income households such as the tasar weavers, women's earnings contribute significantly to family income. In fact, their total earnings, unlike those of their men who spend a part of their income on liquor and such other items, go down to meet the basic need – food – of the family. This underlines the importance of female earnings in these families and hence their crucial need for employment.

Moulik and Purushotham, 1983, p. 274

So far, we have described the various ways in which the heterogeneous groups in poverty may be affected by technical change through the medium of the production system, and in particular, through the alteration in the demand for inputs that is wrought by this process. But as noted above, the impact on the poor will also be transmitted to these groups *qua* consumers, and it is to the nature of this aspect of the issue that we now turn.

Compared to the emphasis on the production aspects of the distributional impact of technological change, very little attention has been paid to the role of consumption. As Scobie (1979, p. 29) has put it,

> The impact of technological change on the distribution of income between producers and consumers *is probably the most powerful and compelling aspect of the distribution consequences*, although ironically, that which receives the scantest recognition in the debate. The benefits which flow to consumers of agricultural products are more diffuse, less visible and often harder to measure than the immediately apparent impact of the income on producers (emphasis added).

It is important to recognize that 'the benefits to consumers' described in this quotation are the result of a fall in the prices of the products that they consume. This way in which consumers benefit is to be distinguished from the improvement of consumption technologies (such as wood-stoves), wherein the gains to consumers arise from an alteration in the nature, or characteristics of the product itself, rather than from a fall in its price. (This distinction is illustrated diagramatically in Figure A3.3 of the appendix to this chapter.)

With respect to the former means by which consumers (rather than producers) may gain, one major determinant is the type of demand for their output faced by producers. At the one extreme is the situation in which demand is such that producers are able to sell as much as they desire without any reduction in the price (so-called perfectly 'elastic demand'). At the other extreme, the market demand is such that prices will fall in response to even a slight increase in production (referred to as highly 'inelastic demand').

In the first case, where there is little or no fall in prices, it is producers rather than consumers who would benefit, while the converse applies to the other polar case (producers and consumers both benefit, of course, from intermediate situations). For a *given* reduction in price, low-income consumers will benefit in proportion to the amount of their budgets that is devoted to the item whose price has fallen. Consequently, a given percentage reduction in the price of say, rice, will yield a substantially greater benefit to the poor than in the case of a less essential item.

EFFICIENCY IN THE USE OF IMPROVED TECHNOLOGIES

The appropriate technology approach implicitly assumes that new technology is efficiently used in production (or consumption, if this is the technology that is improved). But this assumption is most unlikely to be generally true, and will be perhaps most severely violated in relation to changes in traditional technology which demand new and unfamiliar methods of production. The resistance to the new methods that is often imposed by the forces of habit and tradition will tend to imply some degree (which may on occasion be considerable) of inefficiency in the way the new technology is actually used. This point is very well illustrated by the way in which the moldboard plow has been used in India and Pakistan, as described by Johnston and Kilby (1975, p. 423–4, emphasis added).

> Being a specialized implement, the moldboard plow cannot be used for harrowing and intercultivation. Many farmers who have bought a moldboard have not acquired the knowledge, technical skill, and associated implements *to use it effectively*. In fact, they have not infrequently employed it as a wedge in the manner of a local (*desi*) plow. In some areas the techniques used to control bullocks are not very satisfactory so that plowing is not done in a straight line with parallel rows, and the adjustments of the moldboard to reap its benefit are not carried out properly at all.

Examples of inefficient use can also be found among new consumption technologies (such as woodburning stoves[8] and oral rehydration therapy[9]). In general, *actual* as opposed to *potential* gains to adopters from improved technologies are likely to depend, as Figure 3.1 suggests, on the degree of efficiency with which these technologies are used.

adoption → efficiency with which → actual gains to
technology is used   poor

Figure 3.1

On occasion, it may even be the case that the actual benefits derived from improved technology fall short (at least temporarily) of those obtained from the traditional method (although the potential benefits from the former may far exceed those available from the latter).

A further problem is that even if the potential benefits come near to being realized in the short run they may not be maintained in the longer run. Precisely the problems posed by this distinction have been encountered by those concerned with policies for family planning. For a time, it seemed reasonable to these people that initial acceptance of family planning methods would be closely associated with long-term use. Subsequent findings, however, belied this view, since it was found that continuation rates were frequently very low.[10] The same difficulty is described by 'The widespread failure of community water supply and latrine programs, when measured by long-term successful operation or usage' (Kalbermatten *et al*, 1980, p. 22). Indeed, some authors have noted that in some countries, village water systems are breaking down faster than they are being built.[11]

Similar problems have been reported in cases where farm machinery has been introduced at the village level. Several such attempts in Tanzania, for example,

> had required the constant attendance of government workers such as agricultural engineers, with their relatively sophisticated management of, and accounting for, supplies of fuel and spare parts, regular maintenance, and the proper use of machinery. When the government workers were withdrawn, the machinery tended to fall into disuse for lack of one or a combination of these.
>
> MacPherson and Jackson, 1975, p. 103

What a number of these studies emphasize is that a high degree of local involvement is critical to continued, efficient usage. For instance, the explanation of the alarming prevalence of breakdowns and discontinued usage in community well projects, is said to reside in the facts that the community or village has not been adequately involved in the project in the first place, and has not accepted the social responsibility for the task of maintaining the pump.

Darrow *et al.*, p. 53, 1981

Similarly, with respect to sanitation technologies, Kalbermatten *et al.* (1980, p. 30) conclude that

> To result in a successful project, the community's participation should extend from the initial collection of baseline data and identification of user preferences, through the design and construction stage, to the continued operation and maintenance of the facilities. . . . Rural communities . . . need to develop a system they can operate and maintain with a minimum of external inputs.

The discussion thus far has drawn attention to the efficiency and durability of the use that is made of improved technologies, and to the importance of these factors in determining the gains, both static and dynamic, that are realized by a *given* technological improvement. But what may be equally as important, if not more so, is the degree to which the recipients of this technology are able, through changes and adaptations, to continually *improve* its productivity. For without this 'evolutionary' quality (as Jéquier [1976] has called it), any gains from appropriate technology will be merely 'once-for-all' and even these may be negated over time by the technological changes that are occurring in the competing modern sector of the economy. This last consideration leads us to a discussion of dynamic, intersectoral factors.

THE NEGLECT OF DYNAMIC, INTERSECTORAL LINKAGES

We have seen in an earlier section, that what economists refer to as a 'general equilibrium' approach is important to understanding how the benefits of technical change will be distributed in the economy. What is important to this question, that is to say, is not merely what occurs in one sector of the economy, but rather the interactions between the different sectors. Of particular importance in this regard is the impact of changes that occur over time in the *modern* sector on the outcome of policies for technical change in the *non-modern* sector.

What is mainly at issue here (and what tends to be ignored in the appropriate technology approach) is the nature of the relationship over time between the non-modern and the modern sectors. In general, three types of relationships can be identified, namely, complementarity, isolation or non-relationship and competition.

(a) Complementarity

Much has been written about the historically important role of small-scale firms as suppliers of inputs to large enterprises in Japan.[12] In many contemporary developing countries, however, this type of 'forward-linkage' relationship seems to be relatively rare. None of the enterprise surveys in Africa, for example,

> reveal significant sales or subcontracting relationships between the formal sector and small enterprise. In part the manufacture of intermediate and capital goods is constrained by lack of standardization and low levels of quality control. Most small firms in Africa lack the equipment and technical ability to produce standardized inputs for modern industrial firms. But the pattern of import substituting industrialization with its emphasis on assembly operations undoubtedly also constrains the development of specialized small input producers.
>
> Page, 1979, p. 11

The vast majority of the output of small firms is said to go instead to satisfy final consumer demand (especially the demands of the low-income rural and urban populations).[13] Insofar as this is true also of developing countries in other regions,[14] the relations between the modern and non-modern sectors will consequently be better described by one of the other two categories mentioned above.

(b) Isolation

The fact that the major product categories of the small-scale sector (such as clothing and footwear) are manufactured also by large-scale firms in the formal sector does not necessarily imply that a vigorous competitive relationship exists between the sectors. On the contrary, the degree of effective competition may be slight or even non-existent.

One reason is that the products of the two sectors may be highly imperfect substitutes for one another (as measured by the cross-elasticities of demand between them). It is commonly observed for example that the products of small-scale industry are designed to meet the specific needs of low-income consumers in rural areas, whereas firms in the formal sector cater to the different ('high-income') needs of the urban population.[15]

The degree of effective competition between the sectors may also be a function of the adequacy of transport and communications networks (and the corresponding costs of moving goods from one location to another). The sharp contrast in this respect between China and India, for example, is sometimes used to help explain the greater success with which the former has implemented a rural industrialization strategy. In the specific context of the cement industry, Spence makes this argument in the following terms:

> China's policy of decentralised production is encouraged by a much less well-developed transportation network than India has. In China, in order to reach district centres, cement from large centralised plants would frequently need to be transported by road, and transport would add greatly to the price of cement. In India, on the other hand, the extensive railway system enables cement to be transported cheaply all over the country.
>
> Spence, 1978, pp. 21–2

Over time, of course, as transport networks improve in China, competition between the sectors will generally tend to increase. 'At this point local self-sufficiency and initiative will have visible economic costs relative to centralization. Their continuation will require conscious decisions on the part of China's planners' (Perkins, *et al.*, 1977, p. 83). Even then, however, the net benefits from rural industrialization may still be positive from the point of view of China's development goals. This possibility is raised by Perkins *et al.* (1977) in an argument that is based on an eloquent statement of the case for appropriate products. Thus,

> It is not clear that the higher and more consistent quality of sophisticated mills has any significant welfare contribution even if their products tend to command higher prices in international markets. Such markets are not perfect and tend to reflect the purchasing power of Western consuming countries whose values the Chinese reject anyway. High extraction unbleached flour characteristic of the village mills contains more nutrients than the

flour typically produced by more sophisticated mills. Cotton material from rural looms may not be smooth and fine count, but it may be just as durable as that from high-speed looms in urban factories. *In short, the higher labor productivity and technical efficiency of large-scale urban mills may not be sufficient to offset the political and social advantages of small-scale rural mills. If this is the case, then the dual structure of China's agricultural processing industry will exist indefinitely.*

> Perkins, *et al.*, 1977, p. 83, emphasis added

(c) Competition

To the (largely unknown) extent to which the products of the traditional sector compete directly with those of the modern sector and to the degree that the competitiveness between the two is determined by differential rates of technological change, then the challenge that is thereby posed to the successful improvement of traditional technology is a formidable one indeed. For the difficulty is then that the improvement needs to have not merely an ongoing, continuous quality, but also one that is sufficiently dynamic to keep more or less in step with the rate of change in the modern sector (which tends to be rapid because of the dependence of this sector on technological change occurring in the rich countries). Accordingly, the potential of technological improvements for the alleviation of poverty must be judged against this intertemporal criterion as well as their immediate impact on the incomes of traditional producers and consumers.

What occurred in the efforts to upgrade technology in the Indian oilseed processing industry well illustrates the problem that is posed over time by the inherently dynamic pattern of technological change in the modern sector. In particular,

> by the time the technology (power ghani) was improved, the organized sector with its high technology base (baby expellers) moved into the village economy and gained roots. The DS [decentralized sector] found it extremely difficult to sustain itself.
>
> Moulik and Purushotham, 1983, p. 303

More generally it has been observed that,

> any time lag in the development of technology factor relating to a certain sector, particularly the DS, could place it in a highly

disadvantageous position *vis-à-vis* its counterparts. . . . *paying mere equal R&D emphasis toward the technologies of different scale oriented sectors does not ensure a uniform pace in their growth pari passu.* A bit of time lag could turn out to be indefinite drag for the disadvantaged sector.

> Moulik and Purushotham, 1983, pp. 306–7, emphasis added

The Indian experience would seem to point to the need for a small-scale flexible capital-goods sector that is able to produce a continuous countervailing stream of innovations for the sector whose traditional technology has been improved. Much has been made, in this regard, of the importance of the role played historically by a small-scale, dispersed rural capital-goods industry (i.e. backward linkage). Thus, in countries as diverse as Taiwan and China,

> widely dispersed rural workshops manufacturing farm equipment have performed a crucial role as a technological training ground in developing the capacity to build machine tools and other capital goods. This *steady upgrading* of the processes and products of rural industry encourages the development and spread of technologies adapted to a country's factor endowment and thus stimulates continuing growth in the size and competence of its local manufacturing industry.
>
> Johnston, 1981, p. 32, emphasis added

It follows from the two foregoing paragraphs that the viability of improved rural technologies is a function not merely of the immediate competitive relationship confronting these technologies, but also of the conditions that determine whether a vibrant small-scale capital goods sector comes into being. Both of these determinants of viability are likely to be heavily influenced by government policies and in several countries the effect has been to thwart rather than assist such efforts to improve traditional technologies as have been made.

India's policies, for example, by discriminating against the small-scale rural industrial sector, have effectively subverted the efficacy of several attempts to improve traditional technologies in this sector. Thus, according to Moulik and Purushotham (1983, p. 330)

> Some DS [decentralized sector] technologies, though improved, are not able to stand the competition from the highly mechanized, capital intensive sector in terms of productivity and unit costs. . . .

there seemed to be little rationale on the part of the government in not regulating a competing technology and at the same time expressing a strong desire to promote the DS.

Similarly, in the context of the development of small-scale cement plants in India, Spence (1978, p. 49) concludes that

> Even when technical problems have been overcome, the establishment of an alternative technology will be difficult if certain types of support continue to be given to manufacturers of the conventional technology.

These biases in favour of the large-scale cement industry are said to derive from national pricing policy (which makes it difficult for alternative technologies to expand), distribution and freight equalization charges (which reduce the economic advantage of setting up small-scale plants near their markets) and policy towards standard setting (which prevents an adequate but slightly below standard material from being sold).

The last bias – that involving standards – is especially interesting because it offers such a marked contrast with Chinese policy in this area. Specifically, whereas the Indian policy-makers (following developed country practice) rigidly adhered to a single standard, the Chinese defined as many as six different classes of cement.[16] Predictably, these different policies had major implications for the viability of small-scale plants in the two countries.

The abandonment of a small plant in Lucknow is illustrative of what ensued more generally in the Indian case. For although this plant 'produced a cement very acceptable, for most purposes – it failed, on occasions, to satisfy the expansion ratio test specified in the standard' (Spence, 1978, pp. 22–3). In China, in contrast, 'the range of standards available ensures that whatever cement is produced can find some use' (Spence, 1978, p. 22). Low quality cement produced by small plants in the rural areas is thus able, for example, to be used in the construction of dams with earthwork cores (as was noted in Chapter 1).

Government policies have often also run counter to the viability of a small-scale capital goods sector, which, as suggested previously, may be crucial to the sustainability of improvements to traditional technologies. This policy bias can be illustrated with particular clarity in relation to small-scale rural industry in the Pakistan Punjab.

According to Child and Kaneda (1975), the Green Revolution in this area gave rise to a series of production bottlenecks that could easily and appropriately have been met by the products of an indigenous, small-scale engineering industry.

> The threshing machine, which would eliminate the temporary labor shortage at harvest time and permit earlier planting of the next crop, is but the most obvious example. An inexpensive reaper and on-farm storage equipment would make further contributions to productivity. Bottlenecks in land preparation could be reduced by a more efficient plow, and the sowing process improved by a seed drill. . . . In short, there could be substantial backward linkage from agricultural to domestic industry if Pakistan would emphasize a technology based on improved agricultural implements and specific, bottleneck-removing machinery which can be produced by the indigenous, small-scale engineering industry. Both the small independent farmer and the small engineering firm could survive and thrive.
>
> Child and Kaneda, 1975, p. 263

Instead, however, the government chose to adopt a set of macro policies (e.g. heavy public subsidies to capital and import-intensive equipment) which, by favouring the large-scale sector, 'portends not only the demise of the small farmer in the Punjab; it will erode or even erase the market of the small-scale domestic industry supplying capital goods to the agricultural sector' (Child and Kaneda, 1975, p. 263).

Similar observations have been made in relation to India by Johnston and Kilby. They point, on the one hand, to 'rationing policies which deny scarce inputs to small-scale producers of farm equipment and inexpensive consumer goods which have the greatest potential for reaching the bulk of the farm population' (Johnston and Kilby, 1975, p. 451). On the other hand, the policy of underpricing both capital and foreign exchange, which concentrates the agricultural sector's demand for new farm equipment on tractors, threatens to undermine the growth prospects of 'even the more progressive implement manufacturers'. Yet, the Indian experience also contains an instance of the successful creation of a backward linkage to rural industry that appears to have supported, rather than hindered, the sustainability of the upgrading effort. Kaplinsky's study of the upgrading of the OPS sugar technology shows how, during the past decade, this process was accompanied by the emergence of a specialized set of OPS machinery suppliers. 'This has led to their introducing improvements autonomously, and then marketing these to OPS plants' (Kaplinsky, 1983, p. 121). Depending upon the *rate* of these improvements relative to those that occur in the competing VPS sector, the creation of this backward linkage may, therefore, enable a *sustainable* process of upgrading OPS technology to be achieved. But before any lessons for policy can be drawn from this case, much more needs to be known about the particular factors that contributed to its success, in an economic environment that seems generally to discourage this type of favourable interaction.

What evidence is available for Africa, also confirms the contribution of government policies to the widespread failure to effect the beneficial kind of backward linkage that was described in the previous paragraph. Thus, in seeking to explain the 'large gap between the potential contribution of expanded use and local manufacture of simple and inexpensive farm equipment and the actual situation in East Africa', Bruce Johnston (1981, p. 35) has argued that

> Perhaps the most fundamental problem has been a common failure to consider the structural and demographic characteristics of these economies which pose a fundamental choice between a broadly based strategy aimed at the progressive modernization of the great majority of a country's farm households and a 'crash modernization' strategy which concentrates resources in atypically large and capital-intensive farm units.

As in the other countries examined above, that is to say, a widespread and continuous process of technological change seems to be incompatible with a set of policies that have the effect of concentrating available resources among the large-scale units in the agricultural and capital-goods producing sectors of the economy.

CONCLUSIONS

This chapter criticized the view that adoption of improved technologies should be regarded as the ultimate policy goal – a sufficient condition of a successful outcome. It has argued that this view neglects an important range of variables which complicate the impact of adoption on the target group of poor. Depending on the particular configuration of these neglected variables, adoption may or may not help to alleviate poverty.

Much was shown to depend on the differential impact of improved technology on the heterogeneous groups in poverty. In some cases, seemingly appropriate new technologies may leave unchanged or even harm the welfare of the groups that comprise the majority of the poor. In other cases, where it is well matched with the specific composition of the poor in a particular country, technological change will have a far more favourable distributional impact. Much also depends on the extent to which the benefits that are potentially available to the adopter of an innovation are actually realized. For as numerous examples illustrated, new technologies may be used ineffi- ciently, may be poorly maintained or may even be discontinued altogether. The final variable that appears to strongly condition the outcome of technical change is the nature of the relationship over time between the non-modern and modern sectors. Where this relationship is competitive (rather than complementary or non- existent) traditional producers compete with the products of the technologically dynamic modern sector (or with imports). The outcome then depends not only on the intrinsic characteristics of the improved technology but also on government policies that set the context (e.g. prices) in which the competition takes place. It also appears to depend to an important degree on the nature of the backward linkages that are established with a dispersed rural capital-goods sector (which again is in part a function of government policies).

TECHNICAL APPENDIX

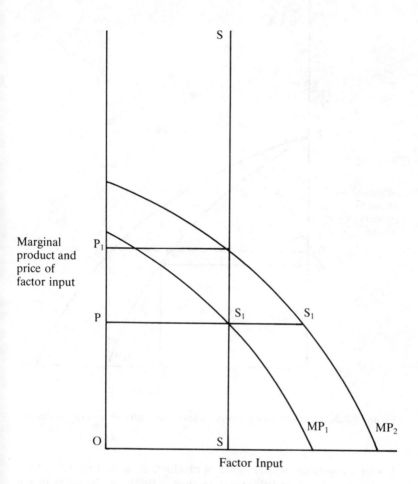

Figure A3.1 *Changes in the demand and supply of factor inputs*

MP_1 is the initial demand curve for the factor and SS the supply curve. The intersection of the two curves yields the price OP. If, after an increase in the demand (and a resultant shift in the curve to MP_2), supply remains constant, the price rises to OP_1. However, if the supply increases along the perfectly elastic curve S_1S_1, the price of the factor will remain constant at OP.

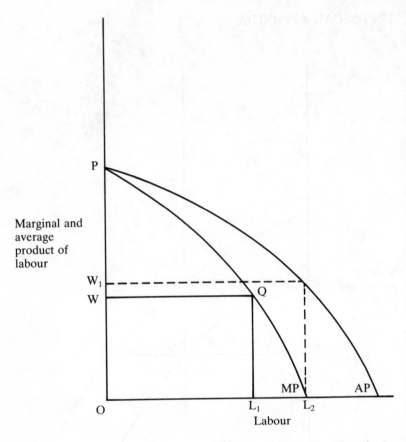

Figure A3.2   *Distribution of income under alternative modes of production*

Under a capitalist (wage) mode of production, with wage OW, OL$_1$
workers are hired and the total product, OPQL$_1$ is shared between
workers (who receive OWQL$_1$) and capitalists (who receive PQW).
Under a non-wage mode of production (e.g. family farms) output will
be pushed to the point where the marginal product of labour is zero
i.e. at OL$_2$. Each worker will receive OW$_1$ (and OW$_1$ multiplied by
OL$_2$ is equal to the total product OPL$_2$).

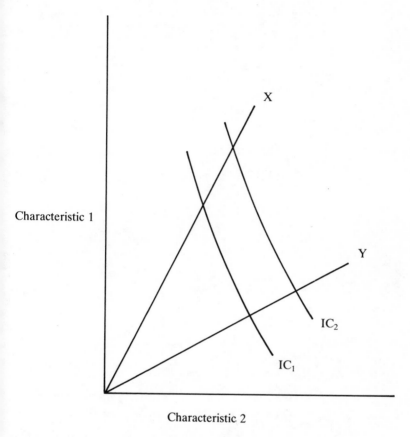

Characteristic 1

Characteristic 2

Figure A3.3   *Upgrading of consumer goods versus a reduction in price of an existing good*

A fall in the price of a given good, X, enables the consumer to buy more of this product, and hence move to the higher indifference curve IC_2. But the movement to IC_2 can also be achieved by the introduction of good Y, which embodies the two characteristics in a different (and preferred) combination from that embodied in good X (i.e. good X is in this sense upgraded to form the new good Y).

4 The Replicability of Development Projects

Chapters 2 and 3 have been concerned with the determinants and consequences of adoption of improved technologies at the project level. As noted in Chapter 1, until very recently the appropriate technology movement has tended to neglect the problem of replicating successful interventions at this level. Defined in a broad way as the reproduction of project ideas, practices and technologies beyond the initial context in which they were introduced and promoted (Weiss *et al.*, 1982), replication is, however, by no means a new concept in development. Indeed, 'The idea of a project as "a demonstration" is as familiar in host government plans as it is in the programs and projects funded by donor agencies' (Weiss *et al.*, 1982, p. 1). There is consequently much that can be learnt from a study of this general experience. What is especially deserving of attention is the fact that the replication envisaged by these many endeavours rarely seems to occur. Consider, for example, Pyle's (1981, p. 13) distressing description of the historical record of replication in development.

> How many times during the last three decades of intensive development efforts has a demonstration or pilot project provided 'the answer' to a development problem? Flushed with enthusiasm and optimism, the model that proved so successful on a small scale is expanded with the hopes of benefiting a larger portion of the population. All too often, unfortunately, the happy story ends there; impact is decreased or disappears completely and in the process officials as well as the public lose confidence and eventually interest in the project-proven approach. Before long the cycle begins again with the testing of a new idea in a small-scale project.

It is becoming increasingly clear that an adequate policy response to the failures alluded to in this quotation cannot be formulated solely within the framework of traditional diffusion research. The reason has to do with the fact that in this framework 'The importance of what happens prior to the beginning of an innovation's diffusion (especially those events that affect the nature of diffusion later on) *has been almost entirely ignored*' (Rogers, 1983, p. 135, emphasis added). For to the extent that these neglected prior stages affect the likelihood of a project innovation being diffused, an exclusive focus on the latter process will entirely mask essential elements of the actual, more complete replication model. Of course, there are occasions (such as when a proven innovation is rapidly taken to the mass market) when the prior stages are relatively unimportant and the outcome of the replication effort does, therefore, largely reflect the success with which the diffusion stage itself is carried out. But in general, the very marked degree of *uncertainty* that attends the replicability of rural project innovations in developing countries means that numerous stages are likely to be required before a decision to diffuse is even undertaken. And if so, it is the manner in which these earlier stages are conducted that will therefore tend to have a crucial bearing on the ultimate outcome of the diffusion process itself.

In this chapter, we shall accordingly review the literature that bears on *all* stages of replication and from the lessons that are derived at each of them it is hoped that a coherent, sequential methodology will emerge. More precisely, the survey will be based on the analytical scheme shown in Table 4.1.

The scheme shown in Table 4.1 seeks breadth of coverage not merely in terms of the need for numerous rows (with diffusion appearing, as suggested above, as only one stage), but also with respect to the range of columns, representing the various implications for replication that are drawn from different perspectives at each stage. The illustrative entries under each column of the matrix are designed to emphasize the general point that replication needs to be conceived of as an inherently multi-disciplinary process, even though, of course, not all the disciplines will be equally represented at every stage.

The studies we shall survey can in principle be classified into one or more of the cells in Table 4.1, and all of them are concerned in different ways to overcome the fundamental problem of uncertainty, that inheres, with varying degrees of severity, at the different stages of projects that seek to replicate elements of themselves on a wide scale. Some of the literature focuses on the uncertainty that attaches to the *demand side* of replication (i.e. on whether demand for the project elements exists or can be made to exist at a wide level), whereas other studies are more concerned with the *supply-side* issue of producing and delivering the project innovation to the widespread group of potential adopters.

Table 4.1 *The analytical scheme of the chapter*

Stage	Operational elements	Economic dimension of replication	Sociological dimension of replication	Political dimension of replication
1. Project design & selection	Design, screening & appraisal of development projects	Simplified *ex ante* cost-benefit analysis		
2. Post-selection & pre-replication	The operation & evaluation of experimental, pilot & demonstration projects		Discerning 'ingredients of success' of pilot project	
3. Replication	a) *Demand Side* The diffusion of information to potential adopters & other ways of influencing demand beyond the project area b) *Supply Side* The production or delivery of replicable project elements to adopting groups beyond the project area			Analysis of nature of political implications of widespread replication of pilot project
4. Post-replication	The measurement & evaluation of the replication outcome (to be used as an input to Stage 1 in future projects)			

PROJECT SELECTION: THE RAMIFICATIONS OF REPLICATION

The stage of screening and selecting projects is of obvious importance since scarce resources have normally to be allocated among projects whose ultimate potential for replicability is at this point especially uncertain. In order to deal effectively with this initially acute uncertainty – and thereby to allocate resources to projects with the highest probabilities of being replicated – it is necessary to determine the variables that bear on the potential for replication of a particular innovation and then to assess the innovation according to the criteria so determined.

In institutions that routinely confront this type of problem (as for example, when private firms have to adjudge the probable replicability of new product ideas), this procedure is normally conducted both informally (through various forms of screening or rating devices) and formally (through some form of cost-benefit analysis). Let us first consider an example of a simple screening procedure for replication.

Screening

Table 4.2 illustrates the sorts of questions that are commonly raised about the replication potential (or equivalent term in marketing parlance), of a new product by business firms in a simple screening format. Following our earlier description of replication as embodying both supply and demand-side aspects, the variables comprising the rows of Table 4.2 have been divided on this basis.

The screening of new product ideas according to the selected sample group of variables shown in Table 4.2 will 'generally be carried out by a multifunctional group or committee so that appropriate inputs from production, finance, R&D, and marketing will be obtained' (Guiltinan and Paul, 1985, p. 190). Innovations then pass or fail the screening for replication according to (perhaps some simple summation of) these informed evaluations or predictions. In the following section, where we deal with more formal means of combining assessments into an overall evaluation of the prospective replicability of an innovation, we also present some detailed guidelines as to how these assessments might be made in the development context of technological innovations for the rural sector.

Table 4.2 *Screening the replication potential of a new product*

A. Demand-side variables

	Very good.	Good.	Average.	Poor.	Very Poor.
Merchandisability	Has product characteristics, over & above those of competing products, that lend themselves to the kind of promotion ... the given company does best	Has promotable characteristics that will compare favorably with the characteristics of competing products	Has promotable characteristics that are equal to those of other products	Has a few characteristics that are promotable, but generally does not measure up to characteristics of competing products	Has no characteristics at all that are equal to competitors' or that lend themselves to imaginative promotion
2. Breadth of market	A national market, a wide variety of consumers, & a potential foreign market	A national market & a wide variety of consumers	Either a national market or a wide variety of consumers	A regional market & a restricted variety of consumers	A specialized market in a small marketing area
3. Place in market	New type of product that will fill a need presently not being fitted	Product that will substantially improve on products presently on the market	Product that will have certain new characteristics that will appeal to a substantial segment of the market	Product that will have minor improvements over products presently on the market	Products similar to those presently on the market & which adds nothing new

Table 4.2 *Screening the replication potential of a new product* (continued)

	B. Supply-side variables				
1. Production knowledge & personnel necessary	Present knowledge & personnel will be able to produce new products	With very few exceptions, present knowledge & personnel will be able to produce new product	With some exceptions, present knowledge & personnel will be able to produce new product	A ratio of approximately 50–50 will prevail between the needs for new knowledge & personnel & for present knowledge & personnel	Mostly new knowledge & personnel are needed to produce the new product
2. Raw materials availability	Company can purchase raw materials from its best supplier(s) exclusively	Company can purchase major portion of raw materials from its best supplier(s) & remainder from any one of a number of companies	Company can purchase approximately ½ of raw materials from its best supplier(s) and other ½ from any one of a number of companies	Company must purchase most of raw materials from any one of a number of companies other than its best supplier(s)	Company must purchase most or all of raw materials from a certain few companies other than its best supplier(s)

Source: Guiltinan and Paul (1985) table 7.4.

Simplified Ex-Ante Cost-Benefit Analysis

Whereas the screening procedure is designed for the most part to evaluate projects in a preliminary, rough-and-ready sort of way, *ex-ante* cost-benefit analysis is a more formal means of assessing the potential for replication of projects that cannot be ruled out on the basis of such preliminary procedures. Both methods, however, belong to the same general class of procedures that attempt evaluation *before* projects are undertaken (and hence the term *ex-ante*), which usually start with a specification of goals and objectives and which then seek to assess the contribution of alternative projects to the attainment of these goals and to assess the costs of attaining the goals under these alternatives (Schuh and Tollini, 1979, p. iv.)

Chambers (1978), Rondinelli (1983) and others are rightly critical of the application of highly sophisticated forms of cost-benefit analysis to problems in developing countries, but these criticisms lose much of their force in relation to the highly simplified versions of this type of analysis, with which we shall here be concerned. In particular, we shall take as a basis, the simple model developed by Easter and Norton in 1977 and try to show how this can serve as a useful framework for assessing and comparing the replication potential of technological innovations in the rural sector.

In the situation envisaged by these authors, there is a proposal to allocate research funds to a programme whose objective is to raise the yield of a particular crop (e.g. corn) and the donor agency is concerned to estimate the cost-benefit ratio of the proposal so as more accurately to assess its claim for inclusion in the annual budget. The basic data required for this estimate are shown in Table 4.3.

Table 4.3 indicates that yields under the programme begin to increase in 1985, and rise to a level 2.25 per cent above the 1975 level by the year 2000 (when the benefits are assumed to terminate). Assuming that total acreage is held constant at the 1975 level, the programme thus generates a gain of 2 bushels per acre (88.9 times 2.25 per cent) or 0.125(2/16) bushels per year for 16 years. This estimate of the benefits, however, is based on the assumption that the innovation will spread across the *entire* area under cultivation (equal to 54 722 000 acres). More realistically, allowance needs to be made for the probability that, say, only 80 per cent of the total area will be affected by the innovation. Even on this reduced area, moreover, the adoption pattern by farmers will exhibit time lags, the expected extent of which, in this example, is shown in Table 4.3 (thus, of the

Table 4.3 Data for the cost-benefit calculation

Cost per annum ($1000)	1975 Yield (bushels/ acre)	1975 Area (1000 acres)	Change in yield by year 2000 (%)	Year available	Rate of adoption			
					1st year	2nd year	3rd year	4th & subsequent years
216.9	88.9	54,722	2.25	1985	30	60	80	80

Source: Easter and Norton (1977) table 1.

entire acreage that is expected to adopt the innovation by the year 2000, 30 per cent will do so by 1985, 60 per cent by 1986 and so on). After allowance in this way for the probability and speed of adoption, the expected annual increment in production can be calculated and when this estimate is multiplied by the assumed price per bushel of $2, the total undiscounted benefits for each year are obtained. Discounting at the (assumed) rate of 10 per cent yields the present value of this future stream of benefits from the programme.

From Table 4.3, total costs of the programme (comprising costs of production, organization and delivery) can be seen to amount to $216 900 per annum and it is assumed that these are incurred over a three-year period. Discounting these costs and comparing them with the present value of benefits provides an overall benefit-cost ratio for the programme of 118.14 (see row 1 of Table 4.4).

Formally, the basis of this illustrative calculation can be expressed in the following general form (of benefits divided by costs).

$$\sum_{t=l}^{n} \frac{\Delta o \times TA \times p \times Rt \times P}{(1+r)^t}$$

$$\sum_{t=1}^{L} \frac{Mt + Dt + Ot}{(1+r)^t}$$

Where, Δo = change in output per acre
TA = total crop area affected by innovation
P = price of output
Rt = per cent of total area which had adopted innovation in year t
p = probability of adoption
l = lag time between implementation of project and adoption
$n - l$ = total number of years for which innovation affects production and/or cost
$Mt, T \& Ot$ = manufacturing, delivery and organizational costs, respectively, in year t
L = total number of years over which costs are incurred
r = discount rate

The sensitivity of the cost-benefit ratio to changes in the values of some of the variables in the equation is illustrated in Table 4.4.

Easter and Norton also provide an estimate which illustrates the pronounced degree of sensitivity of the cost-benefit ratio to variations

Table 4.4 *Sensitivity analysis*
(cost-benefit ratio under various assumptions)

1. Initial assumptions	118
2. With longer lags (i.e. from 7 to 10 years)	102
3. With lower probability of adoption (i.e. from 0.8 to 0.5)	74
4. With both longer lags and lower probability of adoption	64
5. With price of corn equal to $2.50	148
6. With 50% smaller yield increase	59
7. With both lower yield increase and lower probability of adoption	37
8. With lags, probability and yield changed	32

Source: Easter and Norton (1977) table 2.

in the extent of acreage that is affected by the innovation. They show, in particular, that with all else unchanged a decline in the acreage affected from 54.7 million acres (in Table 4.3) to 8.8 million acres, would produce a set of cost-benefit ratios ranging from 5 to 26 (as against the original range of values shown in Table 4.4).

The Implications for Technological Replicability

The exercise that has just been summarized contains a set of powerful implications for selecting (and indeed designing) projects from the point of view of their replication potential. First, the exercise reveals that what is sought from this point of view is not a high value of benefits from the innovation, but rather, a high ratio of benefits to costs. It is almost always likely to be possible, for example, to raise the probability that an innovation will be adopted by increasing the amount that is spent on diffusion/extension, but unless this causes the numerator of the formula defined above to increase more rapidly than the denominator, the *ratio* will fall even though in one sense a greater degree of replication has clearly been achieved. Second, in so far as the benefits from replication themselves are concerned, it is apparent that what is important is not solely the degree of adoption among the producers of a commodity but also that the *commodity itself* should be quantitatively significant in a macroeconomic sense. The benefits from replication, that is to say, may be greater from achieving a low rate of adoption among a small proportion of those producing a major crop than obtaining a very high rate among producers of a relatively insignificant commodity. Related to this point, and third, is the finding that it is the *speed* as well as the *extent* of adoption of an innovation that bears positively on the present value of the benefit stream (i.e. on the numerator of the formula).

Finally, the need for accuracy in the prediction of these variables in any particular case was heavily emphasized in the sensitivity analysis and this predictive accuracy, in turn, requires a detailed understanding of the factors that will predispose the replication variables to take favourable or unfavourable values. Put another way, the challenge is to discern the type of circumstances that are likely to give rise to the rapid diffusion (at low cost) of a highly productive innovation to a high proportion of (a large absolute number of) adopters. (A good example is the motor pump, which, according to Sansom (1969), was rapidly diffused by word-of-mouth throughout the Mekong Delta of South Vietnam in the 1960s, principally because of its profitability to farmers). It is to this difficult task that we now turn, beginning with a discussion of the factors that are likely to conduce to a high probability of adoption.

The Factors Conditioning the Degree of Technological Replicability

(a) The Probability of Adoption Variable

It is obvious that the notion of a 'probability of adoption' only has meaning in relation to a specified group of potential adopters and Weiss *et al.* (1982) have made the useful point that the definition of the latter depends on the particular element of a project that is to be diffused. They suggest, furthermore, that project elements can be divided into three major categories, namely, 'physical elements, including tools; ideas, including those presented in training programs as well as those embodied in practices and technologies; modes of behavior and methods of organizing work, people, territory etc.'(Weiss *et al.*, 1982, p. 17).

The authors point out that elements comprising the first of these categories, namely, those comprising the physical elements of a project (such as tools, energy generating materials and so on) are generally the easiest to identify. The second category, however, presents more serious problems of identification since

> projects often promote changes in behavior that are not associated with specific physical objects. For example, when a project is effective in getting the mothers of young children to be observant about symptoms of particular diseases or the degree of balance in a child's diet, or when a project effort stimulates farmers to work together in groups to procure farm inputs, manage the local

irrigation water supply or market their crops, a change in practice, of the sort implied by this term, has been achieved.

Weiss *et al.*, 1982, p. 18

The third category refers to 'those ideas, attitudes and values which do not necessarily result in the adoption of a specific practice or the use of a specific tool'. And while this category of project elements is inherently the most difficult to identify, it may also – as when a project fosters a sense of confidence at the village level 'about doing things ourselves' – represent an extremely potent source of development.

The relationship between specific project elements and potential adopters is illustrated in the first two columns of Table 4.5 and it is in fact from the specification of these relationships that one may begin to build an assessment of the diffusion potential of a given project.

The third and fourth columns of Table 4.5 link project elements and potential adopters through, respectively, a 'motivation' and an 'opportunity' to adopt. The absence of either of these variables among the category of adopters specified in the second column will, of course, reduce the potential for diffusion of any particular project element.

Thus, for example, if village (A) learns of a well-digging project in village (B) it may simply ignore what has been learned if village (A) has adequate water. The presence of water would suggest that no "motive" exists which would stimulate the adoption of the approaches used in village (B). Similarly, farmers who are aware of the way in which target group farmers are using high-yield seeds will not change their practices if they cannot find a source that can supply them with these seeds.

Weiss *et al.*, 1982, p. 25

Useful as they are, these sorts of exercises based on the chart, only constitute a starting point in the assessment of diffusion potential; in practice numerous factors that complicate the assessment have also to be considered. One such complicating factor derives from the recognition that motivations to adopt technological innovations are frequently multidimensional rather than functions of a single variable (as is mostly suggested in Table 4.5). The motivation to adopt new farming techniques, for example, cannot as Pinstrup-Andersen (1982) has pointed out, normally be expressed solely in terms of their expected profitability. The reason is that

Table 4.5 *Summary of project diffusion potential*

Project element	Potential adopters	Motive	Opportunity
Farming techniques	Other farmers	Income	Information distributed by extension service
Use of gravity in irrigation systems	Other villages	Increased availability of water	Observation
Use of water for household purposes	Farmers & other members of their families where pumps are installed	Convenience & increased supply of water	Experimentation/ word of mouth
Use of gravity to facilitate other 'work'	? villages that see pumps work?	Depends on use	? Demonstrations/ experimentation?

Source: Weiss *et al.*, (1982) table 1.

The anticipated impact (positive or negative) on the achievement of other goals may be of great importance. Among low-income farmers in particular, assurance of a desired crop mix, adequate supplies for home consumption and reasonable family work loads are common and may greatly affect adoption decisions. Thus, failure to consider farm level goals other than profitability in *ex ante* analyses of technology adoption may result in erroneous estimates of the expected adoption rates.

Pinstrup-Andersen, 1982, p. 34

What complicates the analysis further is that each of the various motivations described above may be sensitive in different degrees to diverse aspects of the environment in which the potential adopters are located. In the extreme case, any particular motivation may hold only for the very narrow group of adopters in the area in which the project element is initially introduced. Let us consider first how this general difficulty applies to the motivation based on the expected profitability of an innovation.

What needs to be empirically established in this regard are both the aspects of the environment to which profitability is especially sensitive *as well as the degree to which these environmentally sensitive aspects actually vary in the different locations where potential adopters are to be found.* Table 4.6 is based on the ideas of Binswanger and Ruttan (1978) and illustrates some probable findings in regard to the first of these questions for two different types of technological innovations.

The entries in Table 4.6 reflect the probability that

> Agricultural technologies will be much more sensitive to soil and climate conditions than will industrial technologies which, in turn, may be more sensitive to factor prices. Within agriculture, seed varieties will be more sensitive to the noneconomic environment than will mechanical innovations.
>
> Binswanger and Ruttan, 1978, p. 177

Table 4.6   *The environmental sensitivity of technological innovations*

Nature of sensitivity/ nature of innovation	*Economic factors (e.g. factor prices)*	*Ecological factors (e.g. climate, soil)*
Biological–chemical technology	Low	High
Mechanical technology in industry	High	Low

Once the 'sensitivities' of an innovation have been determined in this way, it becomes necessary to investigate the degree to which these actually vary in environments beyond that of the initial project area. Table 4.7 illustrates the sort of calculation to which this procedure gives rise.

Given this particular set of entries in Table 4.7, it is apparent that the diffusion potential of the technology that is sensitive to the economic environment is considerably greater than the potential of the technology whose sensitivity is principally ecological. As illustra-

Table 4.7   *Environmental variations from conditions found in initial project area*

	Economic (e.g. differences in factor prices)	*Ecological (e.g. differences in soil, climate)*
Area A	Low	High
Area B	Low	High
Area C	Low	High
Area D	Low	High

tive of this type of situation, one can readily point to the ease with which industrial technologies are usually able to be transferred between industrialized countries, in contrast to the pronounced difficulty of effecting transfers of many bio-chemical innovations between different rural areas of the Third World (Binswanger and Ruttan, 1978).

It is considerably more difficult, however, to compare the diffusion potential of technologies according to motivations other than profitability, since the 'environmental sensitivity' of most of these has been much less well-studied. What is clear, though, is that the study of the respects in which many other motivations (such as those listed in the third column of Table 4.5) are sensitive to the environment, is bound to take us into domains well beyond those of economics and ecology with which the previous example was exclusively concerned. The motivation for adoption of consumption technologies, for example, often has to do with non-pecuniary factors which may be sensitive primarily to differences in culture. Take as an illustration of this point the wood-burning stove, among the benefits from the adoption of which could be 'the saving of women's labour time ... the greater ease of cooking, ... the saving of cattle-dung ... and being able to maintain or improve nutritional levels' (Agarwal, 1983, p. 367). These motivations appear to be sensitive to a wide range of socio-cultural variables, such as the status of women within the household (which bears on the question of who makes the adoption decision) and the economic standing of the household (which might influence the degree to which the saving of cattle dung is thought to be important).

Sensitivities of a socio-cultural nature are also likely to be raised in assessing the diffusion potential of various new household sanitation technologies. With respect to double-vault composting (DVC) toilets, for example, a World Bank study has noted that they

> are unsuitable in areas where organic waste matter and grass are not easily available, and where the users do not want to handle or use the composted humus. These factors generally restrict their use to rural or peri-urban areas where users are most likely to have gardens and access to grass for the composting process. Even there, unless there is a strong tradition of reusing excreta in agriculture, DVC toilets have no advantages, and in fact several disadvantages, over the VIP (ventilated improved pit) latrine.
>
> Kalbermatten *et al.*, 1980, p. 6

Further evidence may be taken from the experience with the diffusion of slum upgrading projects. In particular,

Tenure regularization tends to be easiest when slums are located on public land. Upgrading programs usually tackle these areas first. When follow up projects then turn to squatter settlements on private land, tenure regularization becomes a more difficult issue and will generally run into greater political obstacles, longer delays and higher costs.

Baum and Tolbert, 1985, p. 298

In general, therefore, it becomes essential to recognize that

In an agricultural program, the role of economic gains tends to be strong whereas in a health or educational program, the presence of other motivating factors in the environment may have to be sought. In agricultural and industrial programs, the focus of analysis tends to be on the economic and technological segments of the environment. As one moves towards social programs on the other hand, the political and socio-cultural segments of the environment may assume greater relative significance than the purely economic or technological segment.

Paul, 1982, p. 107

Beyond the difficult problems of *identifying* the relevant sensitivities that are highlighted by the examples cited above and of estimating the degree to which these are likely to vary in environments beyond that of the initial project area,[1] are additional complexities associated with the fact that the sensitivities may themselves be susceptible of alteration among the potential adopters. And to the extent that this is the case, assessments of diffusion potential based on the assumption of an immutable environment will be quite unrealistic. In Indonesia's population programme, for instance, the seemingly intractable obstacle to widespread diffusion of family planning techniques that was posed by hostile Islamic opinion, was able to be overcome by a persistent attempt to influence the opinions of influential Islamic leaders (Paul, 1982).

Similarly, there may be economic (e.g. input prices) or ecological (e.g. irrigation) aspects of the environment whose alteration would alter the estimate of the diffusion potential of particular technological innovations. The difficulty, of course, lies in determining exactly which aspects are capable of alteration and which have to be taken as given (because they are set, for instance, by political factors or because their alteration would require more time than is available to the project). In its most general form this difficulty has been described by Hirschman (1967, p. 130) as the 'basic dilemma of project design'. Thus,

> if the project is planned, built, and operated on the basis of certain negative attributes of the status quo, taking them for granted, as inevitable and unchangeable, it may miss important opportunities for effecting positive changes in these attributes – on the contrary, it may even confirm and strengthen them. The achievements of the project would then be far below what they might have been. . . . If, on the other hand, success in the construction and operation of the project is made to hinge on a prior or concurrent or subsequent change in some of the attributes of backwardness, then the project's fate becomes a wager; if the wager is lost, so that the needed change does not occur and the project's success is thereby jeopardized, the project planners will be accused of ignoring local circumstances, traditions and sociopolitical structure and of incorrigible naïveté and lack of realism in general.
>
> Hirschman, 1967, p. 131

While Hirschman points out that there is no general solution to the dilemma (which has necessarily to be resolved on a detailed case-by-case basis), he also indicates that the mere recognition of its existence will tend to improve project design in developing countries. For although, 'the decision which traits to "take", that is, to accept (because they are considered unchangeable) and which ones to make (by changing existing or creating new traits) is crucial to project design and success . . . it is hardly ever spelled out' (Hirschman, 1967, p. 131).

(b) The Speed (Rate) of Diffusion

We took note earlier that the conceptualization of replication ought to include not only the *extent* to which a project element is diffused among the population but also the speed, or rate, with which this occurs. In this regard, there is, as Rogers (1983, p. 7) points out, a popular tendency to assume that 'advantageous innovations will sell themselves, that the obvious benefits of a new idea will be widely

Table 4.8   *The speed of diffusion – a selected sample of past innovations*

	Speed of diffusion	*Extent of diffusion*
A. *Developed Countries*		
Radio (Ironmonger, 1972)	±40 years	From the date of acceleration of consumption to completion of diffusion in the UK
Private cars (Ironmonger, 1972)	±70 years	,,
Television (Ironmonger, 1972)	±20 years	,,
Tunnel oven in pottery industry (Rogers, 1962)	±40 years	From first success to general use
B. *Developing Countries*		
Green Revolution		From introduction to
1. Rice	±12 years	coverage of 44 & 27% of
2. Wheat	±12 years	land areas in developing countries devoted to high-yielding varieties of wheat & rice respectively
Motor pump (Sansom, 1969)	±4 years	From invention date to adoption by approximately two villages in Mekong Delta of South Vietnam
Family planning (Johnston and Clark, 1982)	±7 years	From first trials to coverage of 16 000 villages in Thailand
Irrigation (Bagadion & Korten, 1985)	7 years	From pilot project to replication of 347 projects in the Philippines

realized by potential adopters, and that the innovation will therefore diffuse rapidly'. Yet, 'this is very seldom the case. *Most innovations, in fact, diffuse at a surprisingly slow rate*' (Rogers, 1983, p. 7, emphasis added).

Table 4.8 provides some indication of precisely what a 'slow rate' has meant historically for a selected sample of innovations drawn from developed and developing countries.

Partly on the basis of some of this experience there is a growing recognition that the time horizon within which institutions often expect a wide diffusion of innovations may be unrealistically short. Johnston and Clark (1982, p. 221) for example, argue that

> the funding cycles of both national and international development administrations are much shorter than the time typically required for a development organization to learn its trade. Until and unless these ostensible 'managers' can take a more realistic, longer-range perspective in their program-development efforts, the historical record of overhasty expansions and premature terminations can be expected to continue.

Paul's (1982) study of six cases in which pilot projects were successfuly replicated on a wide scale lends support to this conclusion. For he found that the gradualness with which these replications were conducted actually contributed to their success (for reasons that we explain below).

The validity of these views is, of course, in no way inconsistent with the proposition that the speed of diffusion of *particular* technologies (as well as a given innovation in different circumstances) will vary, and it is to the consideration of these more specific factors that we now turn. These conditioning factors, here as elsewhere in our survey, need to be considered from the standpoint of supply as well as demand.

Demand-Side Factors

By far the most extensive discussion of the demand-side factors that condition the speed with which the diffusion of innovations takes place is to be found in Rogers (1983). By drawing on a wide range of empirical studies (of both developed and developing countries), Rogers is able to isolate a set of variables that best appear to explain observed differentials in the speed with which innovations are diffused. These variables, the meaning that is ascribed to them and the general manner in which they are thought to condition the pace of diffusion are shown in Table 4.9.

In the development context, it is fair to say that the vast proportion of the research in this area has focused on the first category of variables in the table, namely, that dealing with the perceived characteristics of innovations (Feder, Just and Zilberman, 1982). And much of the import of this literature (as noted in Chapter 2) has

Table 4.9 *Variables conditioning the speed of diffusion*

Variable	Interpretation given to variable	Operation of variable
I *Perceived Attributes of Innovations*		
1. Relative advantage	'is the degree to which an innovation is perceived as being better than the idea it supersedes'	'The relative advantage of an innovation, as perceived by members of a social system, is positively related to its rate of adoption'
2. Compatibility	'is the degree to which an innovation is perceived as consistent with the existing values, past experiences, & needs of potential adopters'	'The compatibility of an innovation, as perceived by members of a social system, is positively related to its rate of adoption'
3. Complexity	'is the degree to which an innovation is perceived as relatively difficult to understand and use'	'The complexity of an innovation, as perceived by members of a social system, is negatively related to its rate of adoption'
4. Trialability	'is the degree to which an innovation may be experimented with on a limited basis'	'The trialability of an innovation, as perceived by members of a social system, is positively related to its rate of adoption'
II *Type of Innovation-Decision*		
1. Optional	'are choices to adopt or reject an innovation that are made by an individual independent of the decisions of other members of the system'	'Generally, the fastest rate of adoption of innovations results from authority decisions (depending, of course, on how innovative the authorities are). Optional decisions can usually be made more rapidly than collective ones'
2. Collective	'are choices to adopt or reject an innovation that are made by consensus among the members of a system'	
3. Authority	'are choices to adopt or reject an innovation that are made by a relatively few individuals in a system who possess power, status, or technical expertise'	

Table 4.9   *Variables conditioning the speed of diffusion* (continued)

Variable	Interpretation given to variables	Operation of variable
III Communication Channels	'A communication channel is the means by which messages get from one individual to another'	'mass media channels are often the most rapid & efficient means to inform an audience of potential adopters about the existence of an innovation.... On the other hand, interpersonal channels are more effective in persuading an individual to adopt a new idea'
IV *Nature of the Social System*	'is defined as a set of interrelated units that are engaged in joint problem solving to accomplish a common goal'	'social systems whose members are more closely linked by communication networks have ... a faster rate of adoption of innovations'
V *Extent of Change Agents' Promotion Efforts*	'A change agent is an individual who influences client's innovation decisions in a direction deemed desirable by a change agency'	'The relationship between rate of adoption & change agents' efforts, however, is not usually direct & linear. There is a greater pay-off from a given amount of change agent activity at certain stages in an innovation's diffusion'

Source: Rogers (1983) ch. 6.

been to suggest the rarity with which these conditioning variables (such as 'relative advantage' and 'compatibility') seem to have been incorporated into innovations for the poorest members of rural societies. On the basis of a set of case studies of the East and Southern African experience, for example, Ahmed and Kinsey conclude that 'despite years of R&D in institutions scattered over the region, the small and medium-sized farmers of eastern Africa have yet to experience any real benefits in terms of improved equipment *suitable to their farming circumstances*' (Ahmed and Kinsey, 1984, p. 218, emphasis added).

It is also now apparent that disappointing experiences such as these, can be mostly ascribed to a failure on the part of the institutions concerned adequately to come to terms with the real needs of beneficiary groups. In few places is this important conclusion demonstrated with more clarity than a recent study (Jabbar, 1985) of the differential success with which private and governmental institutions in Bangladesh were able to elicit the needs of potential users of agricultural equipment innovations and the effect that this had on the degree of commercialization of the equipment designs. What is interesting about this study is its description of the different degrees of concern displayed by the two types of institution in actually seeking to uncover user needs. In the formal research institutions

> The researchers hardly ever thought of going to the farmers to ask whether they wanted any improved implement to solve any particular problem. Equipment designs adapted/modified/ developed at formal research stations have been tested at the stations but almost never in actual farm conditions.
>
> A completely different picture was found in the case of designs developed by equipment manufacturing firms. Since their main interest was commercial, they considered farmers' needs and problems as the primary basis of design development.
>
> Jabbar, 1985, p. 13

The results of this disparate orientation to the role of user needs, though predictable, are no less striking: all existing commercial manufacture of equipment derives from private-sector designs and not a single design from the formal research institutions has yet reached the stage of commercial manufacture.

It is in response to this rather extreme, but perhaps not entirely untypical experience, that concern over the need to involve users systematically in the design of publicly-funded innovations has grown in recent years, as reflected, for example, in the now considerable literature on farming systems research. The potential of this approach is sometimes said to derive from its ability *'to increase the efficiency of the resources devoted to developing improved technology*, and the potential gains in terms of improving the livelihood of small farmers' (Norman, 1978, p. 816, emphasis added). In pursuit of this objective, farming systems research embodies the following major methodological components:

(a)   'To develop truly relevant improved technology, it is necessary to recognize the interaction of the technical and human elements. That can best be ensured by the "bottom-up" approach characteristic of farming systems research. This requires a multidisciplinary group working in an interdisciplinary manner' (Norman, 1978, p. 815).

(b)   'There is recognition of the locational specificity or heterogeneity in terms of the technical, exogenous, and endogenous factors' (Norman, 1978, p. 815).

(c)   'The farmer is a central figure in the research process.... his involvement increases the possibility of developing improved systems that will address the constraints he faces' (Norman, 1978, p. 815).

(d)   'The role of the farmer is maximized and reality in the research process ensured by minimizing work on experiment station fields and maximizing it on farmers' fields' (Norman, 1978, p. 815).

(e)   'The research process is recognized as being dynamic and iterative, with backward linkages between farmer and research worker' (Norman, 1978, p. 815).

Particularly in its emphasis on understanding what are often very complex user needs in agriculture, this method seems to approximate the behaviour more often displayed by firms with a commercial motive than by public institutions (as in the case quoted above). But what is not yet at all clear from the many applications of this method in developing countries, is the degree to which its application has actually promoted a more rapid (and widespread) rate of adoption and, if so, whether this increment was obtained *only through higher costs* (Shaner *et al.*, 1982). Indeed, the whole question of efficiency in farming systems research has received remarkably little attention in the literature. This neglect is especially surprising in the light of the 'potentially serious inconsistency between – a farming systems perspective as a holistic view of an often complex farming system and the use of research methods which are cost effective and emphasize rapid results' (Byerlee *et al.*, 1982, p. 899). One way to overcome this difficulty has been suggested by Byerlee *et al.* (1982). They contend that capital-scarce and risk-averse small farmers do not usually make drastic alterations in their farming systems. Instead, these farmers are thought to adopt new practices in a step-wise manner (that is, one or two at a time). Byerlee *et al.* argue that an efficient research strategy should consequently introduce changes on this same (step-wise) basis. And from this proposition follows their view that 'screening of technological alternatives need only focus on changes in key system variables rather than modeling of the whole farming system' (Byerlee *et al.*, 1982, p. 902).

More specifically, they advocate the construction of a simple matrix which has the technological alternatives on one axis and the major system variables on the other. These variables are identified through an exploratory survey, which is based on informal field interviews conducted in a multi-disciplinary manner and guided by a systems view of the farmer's decision-making process. Among the variables that are likely to form part of the matrix are

> profitability, risk, labor use in the peak season, food supplies in the 'hungry' season, or cash expenditures. Brief qualitative or quantitative statements on the impacts of each alternative on each variable form the body of the matrix. With this matrix the researchers can usually judge the few treatments that offer the highest probability for increasing productivity and being accepted by the farmers.
>
> Byerlee *et al.*, 1982 p. 902

From the point of view of *ex-ante* cost-benefit analysis, what is promising about this simplified approach to farming systems research, is that it may enable the probability of adoption variable to be raised *without* a significant increase in the costs of research. To this extent (and there is as yet no evidence on the question[2]) use of the methodology will help to promote technological replicability by improving the allocation of scarce research resources.

Supply-Side Factors

So far, we have looked at the speed of diffusion mostly from the standpoint of potential adopters; that is, from the side of demand. But constraints on the rate at which innovations can be widely spread also have importantly to do with supply, and in particular, with the technical and managerial resources available to those concerned with expanding the scale of an initially very small project. On the basis of his review of six programmes that were highly successful from this point of view – namely, the National Dairy Development of India, the Philippines Rice Development Programme, Kenya's Smallholder Tea Development Programme, the Indonesian Population Programme, the Public Health Programme in China and Mexico's Rural Education Programme – Paul (1982) has forcefully drawn attention to this aspect of the timing of the diffusion process.

Paul's review indicates that in all the cases mentioned, contemporaneous replication all over the country was avoided, and he suggests that the 'phasing strategy' adopted instead was governed by two factors.

> One is the paucity of technical and managerial manpower resources which makes it difficult to cover vast areas all at once. A judgement is being made as to what is manageable given the country's environment and the program's resources. A second consideration is the need to start with segments of a program or region where the chances of success seem most favourable. For a new program that is getting off the ground, this is an important factor both for making the most of its resources and gaining confidence. That the development programs we have reviewed were careful about their phasing strategy seems to have contributed to their successful performance.
>
> Paul, 1982, p. 170

Bagadion and Korten's (1985) study of the phased and successful expansion of a pilot irrigation project in the Philippines is also of relevance in this context. Specifically, Table 4.10 (which is taken from their article), shows how the gradual replication of the pilot project throughout the country was facilitated – and was indeed made possible – by the proportionate expansion in the supply of personnel through extensive training and workshop courses.

(c) The Costs of Diffusion

Much of the literature tends to emphasize the benefit side of diffusion and to neglect the corresponding cost dimension (a tendency that we observed, for example, in relation to farming systems research). Yet, at an early stage of the chapter the point was made that a useful concept of replication involves the latter as much as it does the

Table 4.10 *Phased replication of a pilot irrigation project*

Year	Projects Number added	Hectares covered	Workshops and training courses Number	Participants
1976–8	1	400	1	25
1979	2	550	2	75
1980	12	1800	6	150
1981	24	3600	36	600
1982	108	16200	50	1700
1983	200	30000	60	2000
Total	347	52550	135	4550

Source: Bagadion and Korten (1985) table 3–1.

former. Moreover, as the examples cited in this section clearly indicate, the cost side of this equation is sensitive to variables that, in part at least, admit of influence by project planners.

1. Beneficiary Involvement

Particularly where project elements have to be diffused to a heterogeneous (physical, cultural or economic) environment, involvement of beneficiaries in the diffusion process may have a highly favourable impact on costs. Both the Indonesian Population Programme and the Chinese Public Health Programme, for example, had to contend with vast regional diversities that demanded a highly cost-effective delivery service if programme benefits were to be widely spread. In the case of the former, for example,

> Given the magnitude of eligible couples to be reached (14 million in Java and Bali in 1974) and the number of villages to be served, it would have been an uphill task for the government to provide the needed services exclusively through the official structure and personnel. The funds and trained manpower would be immense, whereas the resources available were limited.
>
> Paul, 1982, p. 67

Fortunately, both programmes were able to mobilize systems of local organization that were already in place and the intensive use of these 'readily available resources' constituted a highly cost-effective solution to the delivery problems described above (Paul, 1982).

The point of these and other similar examples (the Philippines irrigation project described earlier in Table 4.10 could also be cited in this context), is not to suggest that local involvement is necessarily a cost-effective mode of diffusion of project elements. On the contrary, because bringing about participation may be highly costly, this approach may often represent an inefficient alternative. The point is rather that where they exist, local organizations can and should be considered as a resource to be exploited in the interests of achieving maximum diffusion benefits from a given level of costs. And it perhaps bears emphasizing that the usefulness of these social organizations may not always be immediately apparent to project planners, a point that is very nicely illustrated in a highly successful settlement project in Senegal.[3] Contrary to what the designers of this project had expected,

the participants went right on using their ancestral social organiza-tion and transferred their extended kinship networks to project lands . . . this spontaneous use of extended family ties . . . proved so effective that the ex post evaluation called it 'triggered settlement' and suggested it be replicated in other West African projects. The audit considers triggered settlement cost effective because in a kin-based society the extended family networks attract additional settlers and therefore foster spontaneous settlement. The report cites a village study showing that twice as many people as estimated are benefitting from the project because members of the extended families of the original settlers have joined them in the project area.

Kottak, 1985, pp. 334–5

2. Population Density

Boserup (1982) and others have emphasized that the costs of providing infrastructural services (such as health, education, etc.) to rural areas, tend to be an inverse function of population density (i.e. numbers per land unit). Studies of infrastructure in urban areas often make the same point: in India, for example, infrastructure for industry costs 13 per cent more in a town of 50 000 than in a city of a million (Gillis *et al.*, 1983, p. 555).

It follows from this hypothesized relationship that a *given* expendi-ture for diffusion will be most effectively devoted to areas of high density.

It has been suggested that to have a reasonably efficient extension system, the extension agent should be located in a town of at least two thousand and should serve an agricultural population of at least five thousand, which should be within a seven-kilometer distance from the center if rural roads are poor and foot and bicycle transport the main means to reach the producers. If we accept these figures, at least seven thousand should live less than seven kilometers from the center.

Boserup, 1982, p. 204

Whether or not one agrees with the particular figures cited in the quotation, the general implication is an important one and one which recently received some support from the findings of a study which concluded that,

The most successful irrigation projects reviewed for this report tended to be located in more densely populated areas (as were traditional irrigation systems). Extension and implementation are facilitated when people are more concentrated and easier to reach.

Kottak, 1985, p. 347

(d) Productivity Change

The numerical example based on Table 4.3 above, oversimplifies, in a number of important ways, the issues that are raised by productivity change in *ex-ante* cost-benefit analysis.

In the first place, although productivity (in the specific form of yield per acre) has an independent status in the formula based on that table, it also plays an *instrumental* role in determining the benefits from diffusion, because of its influence on several of the other variables in the formula that we have already discussed. Through its impact on profitability, for example, increased productivity implicitly forms part of the discussion on the motivation to adopt innovations that we undertook in connection with the probability of adoption variable. By being part of what Rogers refers to as 'the relative advantage' of an innovation (see Table 4.9), moreover, productivity increases are among the determinants of the rate of adoption. In fact, it is precisely to the problem of discovering yield-limiting factors in specific farm environments that a good deal of farming systems research has been devoted.[4]

The second respect in which our example oversimplifies matters stems from the fact that it is concerned with changes in the productivity of only *one* factor, namely, land. In reality, however, resource allocation decisions have, to an important degree, to be concerned with the problem precisely of *choosing* the factors whose productivity is to be raised. This wider issue has been discussed mostly in relation to Hayami and Ruttan's induced innovation hypothesis, which 'has strong and clear implications for the allocation of research resources to factors of production' (Binswanger and Ryan, 1977, p. 223). The hypothesis implies, in particular, that the highest pay-off (in terms of efficiency) can normally be expected from an allocation that seeks to increase the productivity of (or save) factors in relatively scarce supply. 'Thus, in societies with high unemployment and with very limited possibilities of expanding the agricultural area, research priorities should attempt to develop technology that is labour using and land saving' (Pinstrup-Andersen, 1982, p. 196). Though this is in fact frequently the type of innovation that is indicated by the hypothesis, it is by no means a universal prescription. For not only are there many parts of the Third World in which (at certain times) labour is the *scarce* resource, but there also are areas in which land is relatively plentiful.

THE POST-SELECTION, PRE-REPLICATION STAGE: IMPLICATIONS FOR REPLICABILITY

Even if the principles described in the previous discussion of *ex-ante* cost-benefit analysis are used to select projects with a high potential for replication, it will not normally be prudent to proceed immediately to this ultimate stage in the process. For as noted above, except in a narrow set of circumstances, a considerable degree of uncertainty will still attend the (probable success of the) new project, and this feature will require that the project be introduced on an initially small scale.

> Smallness is essential for two reasons: economics and ease of abandonment. A considerable investment in time and resources is essential to start pilot programs. In the state of ignorance that exists when an experiment begins, it is better to test it on a small scale than a large one. This prevents excessive investment in models that may not yield beneficial results. Additionally, if data indicate that the pilot program does not work, ... it can be abandoned with more ease than if it had been initiated on a large scale.
>
> Fairweather and Tornatzky, 1977, pp. 30–1

Obvious and sensible though this suggestion may seem to be, it has not, however, invariably been followed in development practice. Paul, for example, has noted that 'In many countries, *national* programs are launched in a hurry without any concern for developing and testing the relevance and feasibility of the service being replicated' (Paul, 1982, p. 228, emphasis added). In a specific example of the costliness of this type of ill-advised replication procedure, Weiss *et al.* report that

> a soybean project in Central America sustained significant losses during its production phase when peasant farmers harvested the beans by slicing the vines with machetes rather than using the special combines designed to cut and shell the beans. A pilot test covering the plant cycle from seed to harvest would have been one means of avoiding such a loss on a large scale.
>
> Weiss *et al.*, 1977, p. 97

Enhancing the Replicability of Small-Scale Projects

It is one thing to recognize the essentiality of 'smallness' to the avoidance of outcomes such as this; it is quite another to establish how this feature may be used to *promote* the ultimate replicability of projects (or project elements). In this part of the chapter, we shall suggest that an enhanced replication of small-scale projects requires the recognitions that: (a) there are different types of this class of project, (b) the modes of enhancement operate differentially according to these various project types.

Differentiating Between Small Projects

Following a number of authors (Rondinelli, 1983; Pyle, 1980 and Weiss *et al.*, 1977), a distinction can usefully be drawn between experimental, pilot and demonstration projects. The first two of these categories are concerned, in different ways, with the testing of projects. Experimental projects may be said to involve testing in the broad sense of increasing knowledge about some element of a project through field experience. Pilot projects, in contrast, are concerned with testing in a very much more *specific* sense. In particular, the objective of this type of project 'is to test an approach on a representative sample of a given population to determine whether that approach can be successfully implemented in a larger setting' (Cuca and Pierce, 1977, p. 39). The knowledge that is sought from this form of test, that is to say, is purely *evaluative* and is to be derived from the application of the standard scientific method.

While the distinction between pilot and experimental projects thus turns on the *type* of knowledge that they seek to generate, demonstration projects are only in part concerned with testing. The main objective of this third category of projects is rather 'to exhibit new techniques and to diffuse practices which promise wide applicability leading to increased output, superior quality output, or both' (Weiss *et al.*, 1977, p. 99). Demonstration projects often occur after the pilot and experimental phases, and in terms of size and an emerging concern with replication, these projects begin to take on the appearance of aspects of the replication stage itself. But demonstration projects nevertheless retain also an affinity with the other project types in so far as they facilitate the testing of project aspects that are often not discernible at a smaller scale (examples of which are given below). 'In effect, more of the system is tested in demonstration projects because logistics and support mechanisms, a full range of personnel, and other needs must be met to integrate all of the organizational and physical inputs for a full province-level project' (Weiss *et al.*, 1977, p. 99).

While, therefore, it is true that there are certain similarities between the various types of projects that comprise the pre-replication (or, as it is sometimes called, program) stage, there are also fundamental differences. When these differences become blurred (as is often the case), unfavourable implications for replication ensue, because the chances of success of the *initial* project (which provides the elements to be replicated) are thereby undermined. Pyle's (1980) study of Project Poshak in India provides perhaps the clearest demonstration of this important point.

Project Poshak, an integrated health and nutrition project in Madhya Pradesh, began as an attempt to 'evaluate the operational feasibility, efficiency, impact, and economics of an integrated health-nutrition scheme' (Pyle, 1980, p. 125). The different institutions involved in the project, however, adopted different views of quite what the initial project was intended to achieve. Whereas the state government, for example, was principally interested in a pilot project, CARE (one of the other institutions involved) seemed to hold a conception of the scheme that was closer to a demonstration or experimental project. These and other contrasting conceptions made it difficult for those involved to identify what the outcome of the project was to mean. Moreover, it complicated practical decisions since participants were often at odds with one another. Most importantly, the state government saw its primary interest in a pilot study being obscured by a research-cum-demonstration project that did not serve its purposes.

Pyle, 1980, p. 133

The Modes of Enhancement of Replication

It was suggested immediately above that a clear statement of the objectives of a small-scale project will avoid the type of confusion and disillusionment that (as in the case of Poshak) help to undermine its success (and by extension, also, its ultimate replicability). But it is also essential to recognize that corresponding to the particular objective specified, is a set of proposals for directly enhancing project replicability. Table 4.11 summarizes these proposals and gives a few examples of each.

1. Pilot Projects and the Evaluative Mode

As noted above, the objective of a pilot project is not to prove that an innovation can be made to work; the goal, rather, is to secure a project design which is such that *if the pilot turns out to be successful, one can be confident, within reasonable and known limits, of its replicability on a wide scale*. Replication, that is to say, is enhanced here through a purely *evaluative* mode.

The general pilot-design requirements for this form of enhancement have been succinctly stated by Cuca and Pierce in the following terms.

> The ability to generalize results depends on the external validity or representativeness of the experimental design. Has the population studied been randomly selected? Were there controls for the reactive effects of testing and the interactive effects of selection biases and the experimental variable. Replicability is also contingent on operational validity, that is, use of resources in the experiment must be replicable within a regular program, and the approach and sponsorship must be acceptable in a broader context.

Cuca and Pierce, 1977, p. 39

Table 4.11   *Modes of enhancement*

Project type	Objective(s)	Mode of replication enhancement	Examples
1. Pilot	Testing on small-scale to determine likelihood of success on larger scale	Evaluative (i.e. to evaluate the project in an 'optimal' (or scientifically sound) manner	Auxiliary Midwives Project in Thailand (Cuca and Pierce, 1977)
2. Experimental	Testing to acquire knowledge of project	Learning (i.e. promoting the integration of initial & diffusion stages by using former as means to build up capability to implement latter)	India's Dairy Development Programme (Paul, 1982); Participatory Irrigation in the Philippines (Bagadion and Korten, 1985)
3. Demonstration	Convincing others that project can be made to work/ diffusion/testing of certain aspects of project	Gaining political & other support/ promoting diffusion/ evaluation of project at a larger scale than under 1. or 2. above	Masagana-99 (the Philippines Rice Development Programme, Weiss *et al.*, 1977); integrated health, nutrition & family planning projects in Maharashtra (Pyle, 1981)

Of course, the relevant experimental dimensions that are to be controlled in this way will vary from one project to another. Not all projects, for example, use the same material inputs, nor do they all confront the same dimensions (religious, cultural, political, etc.) of acceptability. But whatever the essential dimensions happen to be, the valid generalization of the project to the level of society as a whole depends crucially on achieving representativeness on each of them. In a useful and specific illustration of this point, Fairweather and Tornatzky (1977) consider the reduced generalizability of a project that results from the failure to achieve 'perfect' representativeness in only one out of three dimensions. They show, in particular, 'a dramatic drop of 50% generalizability [from the complete level] when two dimensions are perfectly representative and one dimension is only 50% representative' (p. 348).

Attainment of the experimental ideal which was described in the previous paragraph, and which would facilitate replication through the controlled evaluation of the pilot project, has, in development practice, confronted a number of severe difficulties that may be classified under the following general headings.

(a) Environmental difficulties: On occasion, difficulties in establishing controlled experiments arise from the nature of the environment in which the project is located. In Kenya's Special Rural Development Programme, for example, 'it was difficult, if not impossible, to establish valid experimental and control groups in each area. Different ecological, social, economic and physical conditions made comparison difficult even in relatively homogeneous regions' (Rondinelli, 1983, p. 93).

(b) Cost constraints: In many other cases, the sheer costs of conducting experiments along rigidly controlled lines have rendered infeasible this form of approach. Cuca and Pierce's review of family planning projects, for example, notes that

> Cost might also have been a deterrent to implementing the methodological lessons of earlier experiments. Although a more sophisticated methodology might have enhanced the validity of the results, the additional expense might not have been justified if the broad objective of an experiment could be achieved with less sophistication.
>
> Cuca and Pierce, 1977, p. 71

(c) The difficult choice of project duration: Several authors have drawn attention to the dangers of generalizing from a successful pilot scheme that is of only brief duration.

> For example, if a model is put into operation and a 'successful' outcome is achieved only for a single 90-day follow-up period and then only on one dependent measure, inferences should be conservative. If the "success" were used as the basis for a massive national implementation effort, the results are likely to be extremely unfortunate. . . . If success is achieved in 90 days and again in 180 days and in one year and once more in two years, the

experimenter can say with considerable confidence that the social model is a true long-term success.

Fairweather and Tornatzky, 1977, p. 31

Moreover, the very novelty of short-run projects may enable them to be successful over this period (but not, of course, over the longer run).

While they may help to overcome these problems, pilot projects of longer duration tend, however, to create problems of their own. These arise not merely from the costs of extended duration but also from the methodological difficulties that are associated with the extension itself. In particular, 'experiments of long duration may be subject to interference from other factors in the experimental environment. Such phenomena as significant socioeconomic development may jeopardize the precise measurement of the effect of the intervention' (Cuca and Pierce, 1977 p. 7).

(d) The inherent bias to succeed: The development literature abounds with examples of small-scale projects in which far more resources are employed than could conceivably be replicated on a national scale. Writing in 1965, Hapgood, for example, observed that

> When one examines existing pilot schemes, one typically finds a very high extension-farmer ratio: a relatively great number of skilled people is being used to provide new knowledge and services to relatively few farmers. Usually the manpower is not available to generalize the scheme at that ratio, and it may not work at a lower ratio of skilled people to farmers.

Hapgood, 1965, p. 124

More recently, Cuca and Pierce encountered the same tendency in certain family planning experiments, which, 'employed resources that simply could not be duplicated within a regular program' (Cuca and Pierce, 1977, p. 41). They cite particular examples of projects in Pakistan and India, whose initial success – because it was predicated upon the employment of disproportionately large numbers of workers – necessarily could not be replicated on a larger scale.[5]

In part, of course, this observed propensity for projects to embody resources in initially disproportionate amounts can be explained by the fact of their design as demonstration rather than as pilot projects. But even in instances where small-scale projects are *not* explicitly conceived in this way, the same systematic bias is often discernible. Consider, for example, what occurred in Project Poshak, a case to which we have already alluded.

> Despite the fact that the project was initiated with the explicit intention of operating within the existing infrastructure, this proved not to be possible. While no new personnel were hired for the project, all the participating health centers were brought up to full authorized strength by transferring personnel from nonparticipating health centers. As a rule at this time in India, several staff positions in all health centers were left unfilled. Thus, the health facilities of Project Poshak were exceptional to start with; this situation would make the system difficult or impossible to duplicate if fully staffed centers were thought to be essential for the success of the scheme. Moreover, the staff spent considerably more time than was originally allotted to carry out Poshak work. Most workers spent either a high percentage or all of their time on the integrated program, and as a result, had to neglect some of their other duties.
>
> Pyle, 1980, p. 131

What occurred in Project Poshak appears, in at least some degree, to be part of a 'success syndrome' that is not unfamiliar to observers of the motivational aspects of small-scale development projects. Brandt and Cheong, for instance, in the context of community-based planning in the rural areas of South Korea, write of a 'compulsion' to do everything possible to ensure the success of a project,

> regardless of comparative needs elsewhere. The success of that particular initiative becomes almost an end in itself.... The Coordinators personal sense of mission and identity as well as his career reputation are linked to successful project completion in one particular context. And to some extent this phenomenon is reinforced at higher levels.
>
> Brandt and Cheong, 1980, p. 614

(e) Variables that are not subject to experimental control: In so far as replication involves simply the proportionate scaling-up of all relevant variables, experimental control can in principle (if not always in practice, as we have seen) be exercised. But replication may often amount to more than this mere process of scalar enlargement,

because, as Hapgood puts it, 'There is a difference *in kind* – not just *in scale* – between a pilot and a national scheme' (Hapgood, 1965, p. 123, emphasis added.) If, in other words, the whole (in this sense, replication) has to be conceived differently from the sum of its component parts (the small-scale projects), then it is clear that the experimental method ceases to retain its efficacy.

There are several aspects to this difficulty. One is that 'Administrative problems which might remain hidden in a small-scale effort are more likely to surface in larger undertakings' (Cuca and Pierce, 1977, p. 42). Similarly, at the political level 'Bureaucratic opposition, skirted at the pilot stage, may arise when the scheme becomes large enough to be perceived as a threat to the customs or status of the civil service' (Hapgood, 1965, p. 124). A third aspect is economic and involves what economists refer to as 'the fallacy of composition'. That is, the aggregate effects of a policy differ from the micro effects.

> For example, one small farmer may benefit from rural education and extension programs, cheap capital, and subsidized farm inputs. *If the program is expanded on a large scale, however, the resulting decrease in farm prices may be so great that it reduces the income of small farmers.*
>
> Frank and Webb, 1977, p. 24, emphasis added

In a later section, it will be suggested that the general class of problems to which these examples relate, namely, those which emerge only at a particular scale of operations, appear to comprise an essential component of the transition to widespread replication. And in that section we shall also describe the varying degrees of success with which some of these scale-specific problems have been confronted in practice.

2. *Learning Through Experimental Projects*

Even if all the previously mentioned practical problems of applying the experimental method to pilot projects could be overcome, there are some authors who would still be reluctant to adopt this approach as a general model for enhancing replication.

Johnston and Clark (1982), for example, have argued that the experimental method is applicable only to particular types of projects.

This is certainly the case when an extension service wants to evaluate the growth potential of a new rice variety. It is likewise credible when a new oral-rehydration technique is being field 'tested' for the first time. In such cases, the experiment is clearly defined, and the learning is properly accruing to the senior facilitator people who will be responsible for revising or distributing the tested innovation.

Johnston and Clark, 1982, p. 223

But in what are arguably the majority of cases, the learning experience needs to accrue, instead, to the local participants in the project. In such cases, that is to say,

program success requires that the local people and their field-level facilitators learn how better to organize themselves to deal with a continuing problem area. All too often, this distinction is overlooked by planners or donors intent on 'demonstrating', 'testing', or 'proving' the merits of a particular blueprint for subsequent program organization. Temporary staff and structures are brought in to assure program success and an adequate control of presumed key variables. *The result is that the learning accrues to the wrong people*. Once the experiment is completed ... leaving the local groups as ignorant and inexperienced as they were to begin with.

Johnston and Clark, 1982, p. 223, emphasis added.

The absence of mechanisms to promote local learning is of concern also to Bagadion and Korten (1985), who emphasize the role in this of bureaucratic imperatives. They point, in particular, to the disbursement schedules facing the staff that is responsible for overseeing the small-scale project and suggest that these schedules sometimes dictate 'a pace too fast to allow a thoughtful examination of the small-scale pilot project' (Bagadion and Korten, 1985, p. 84). Bagadion and Korten argue, furthermore, that even if mechanisms (such as specially formed groups) were available to extract from the initial project 'the knowledge for developing broader implementation capacities', any knowledge thus acquired would be unhelpful to the extent that the small and main projects are simultaneously pursued. For then, by the time the accumulated knowledge by the former becomes available, 'the personnel on the other parts of the project have usually already pursued their own approaches' (Bagadion and Korten, 1985, p. 84).

Taken together, the view that replication often requires an enhancement of local capabilities and the recognition that the mechanisms for this are not likely to inhere in the usual run of project design, has prompted an alternative approach, one that has learning as its raison d'être.

The learning process approach to replication In Korten's model (Korten, 1980) learning is built explicitly not only into the initial experimental phase of the project but into all its subsequent phases as well. 'In each stage the emphasis is on a different learning task, successively on *effectiveness, efficiency, and expansion*' (Korten, 1980, p. 499, emphasis in original). From the first stage in this scheme, in which effectiveness emerges out of a trial and error process described as a 'village level learning laboratory', the idealized sequence proceeds through to Stage 2, wherein, 'Through careful analysis of Stage 1 experience, extraneous activities not essential to effectiveness are gradually eliminated and the important activities routinized' (Korten, 1980, p. 500). It is also at this stage that some 'modest' degree of project expansion is called for in order to provide learning-by-doing experience to personnel, which may then be used for strengthening the organizational capability required for Stage 3. It is, in fact, the rate at which this capability can be made to expand that largely sets the pace at which the final, learning-to-expand phase culminates in 'a relatively stable, large-scale operation'.

Korten compares this learning process model with what he calls the 'blueprint approach', in which emphasis is laid on 'well planned and clearly defined projects and visible outcomes', and he suggests that the former rather than the latter, underlies some of the few instances of successful replication that have occurred in Asia. With reference specifically to the Indian National Dairy Programme, the Sarvodaya Movement in Sri Lanka, the Bangladesh Rural Advancement Committee, the Thailand Community Based Family Planning Services and the Philippine National Irrigation Administration Communal Program, the argument is made that

the blueprint approach never played more than an incidental role in their development. These five programs were not designed and implemented – rather they emerged out of a learning process in which villagers and program personnel shared their knowledge and resources to create a program which achieved a fit between needs and capacities of the beneficiaries and those of the outsiders who were providing the assistance. Leadership and teamwork, rather than blueprints, were the key elements.

Korten, 1980, p. 497

On the basis of a different, but overlapping sample, Paul (1982) arrives at a conclusion that has much in common with this interpretation of the five Asian cases. Paul's case-studies (to which reference has already been made) indicate, as do Korten's, not only the instrumental role of experimental projects in the learning process, but also the importance of this process to the success with which the transition to widespread replication is made. In particular,

> It is significant that those who managed the programs had an active role in the pilot project planning and operations. Pilot projects were not viewed as a separate activity to be left to researchers. The interaction between the people engaged in pilot projects and the national programs was very strong. The managers and implementors were thus able to internalize the lessons effectively and were motivated to use them in their strategic planning.
>
> Paul, 1982, p. 169

Taken together, the results of the studies by Paul and Korten[6] contain powerful implications for the design of experimental projects as part of a replication strategy. Many of these implications, as both authors are concerned to emphasize, involve a quite substantial departure from current institutional practices and procedures.[7] For one thing,

> the conventional practice of isolating pilot projects and experiments from national programs needs to be discouraged.... governments ought to ... integrate pilot projects with national programs organically rather than view the two as discrete parts linked indirectly through administrative fiat.
>
> Paul, 1982, p. 242–3

From the point of view of funding agencies as well, certain fundamental changes are thought to be in order.

> For example, a portion of their funding portfolios might be programmed not around sectors, but around individuals with the leadership qualities, the ideas, and the commitment to advancing the cause of rural people from which substantial programs might be built. This would provide the recipient change agents with the flexible funding which might allow them over a period of five to ten

years to carry their idea through the three development stages to the building of a major mature program.

Korten, 1980, p. 502

Because the initial investment, on this view, is akin to a high-risk, venture-capital commitment, Korten proposes that

working with programs through Stages 1 and 2 should probably be limited to relatively smaller donors with highly qualified field staff, substantial programming flexibility, and no qualms about taking on high risk, staff-intensive activities.

Korten, 1980, p. 510

Stage 3 programmes (and programmes that have moved beyond this stage), in contrast, are thought to be better suited to larger donors.

3. Promoting Acceptability Through Demonstration Projects

The final mode of replication enhancement shown in Table 4.11 refers to demonstration projects, the principal objective of which was described earlier as being to promote, rather than test, innovations. As such, these projects are usually based upon the prior results of tests conducted as part of pilot or experimental approaches.

The Masagana-99 rice programme in the Philippines, for example,

was implemented through the experimental and pilot stages, then put into operation in selected provinces on a demonstration project basis.... By mobilizing political and agency support at all levels from governor to extension agents and farmers, North Cotabato became the second highest producing province in the country... The success of the demonstration projects in this province and others has laid a basis for dissemination of results more widely.

Weiss *et al.*, 1977, p. 99

The Masagana example draws attention to several of the most important ways in which demonstration projects may serve to promote replication. One is through the mobilization of political support, without which (as the Chilalo Agricultural Development Project in Ethiopia demonstrated),[8] the project is unlikely to be capable of more than only very limited spread. The precise manner in which this mobilization is sought, will, of course, vary from one circumstance to another. However, on the basis of his experience with a sample of demonstration projects in India, Pyle has usefully suggested a set of guidelines as to how political support might, more generally, be garnered.

He advocates, firstly, that the base of support within the govern-ment be broadened. There is need not only to reduce dependence on a single government official (and thereby to provide more administra-tive continuity) but also, to improve the project's visibility. 'Because pilot projects do not receive much attention, this added support could be very important when it comes to discuss the scheme's long-term future' (Pyle, 1980, p. 143). In so far as this 'added support' is insufficient, however, Pyle suggests, secondly, that 'more in the way of publicity is required in order to build up a constituency for the scheme. *Aggressive public relations efforts during the fieldwork are a necessary part of a pilot project's life if eventual adoption is an objective* (Pyle, 1980, p. 143, emphasis added). The third, and perhaps most frequently neglected proposal offered by Pyle is what he refers to as 'selling the concept'. That is to say, 'The approach must be packaged to make it appeal, very much the way a new product might be marketed' (Pyle, 1980, p. 143). In general, and following the analogy of the marketing of a new product, this can most effectively be achieved if the project is cast in terms that are appealing to the government. 'If, for instance, the government had a great interest in family planning or increased utilization of health centers, program promoters would be advised to stress these features of the project' (Pyle, 1980, p. 144).

The second (and related) aspect of demonstration projects to which the apparently successful Masagana experience in the Philip-pines draws attention, is the 'demonstration effect' itself and the attention that needs to be given to its realization. If the project, that is to say, is truly to be able to demonstrate the virtues of an innovation (to potential adopters, government officials, etc.), it is essential that the operational conditions be such as to facilitate this task. In many cases, the importance of this point is recognized in the implementation of demonstration projects. For example, 'The expe-rience with integrated agricultural development projects in India indicates that careful site selection was a crucial factor in promoting new farming methods' (Rondinelli, 1983, p. 106). Similarly, in South Korea's community-based rural planning initiative, it is acknow-ledged that without relatively rapid and tangible progress in the project areas, 'neither the local population nor the Korean Government is going to become enthusiastically involved' (Brandt and Cheong, 1980, p. 615). In other cases, however, the choice of environment for the demonstration project appears to have hindered, rather than promoted, the achievement of its objective. With regard to the choice of Madhya Pradesh as the location for the demonstration of health and nutrition schemes as part of Project Poshak, for instance, Pyle has raised the question of whether a 'more progressive state' would have been more suitable. His argument is precisely that 'once the Poshak concept had succeeded and had been adopted in a more advanced state, the poorer states like Madhya Pradesh would have stood a better chance of eventually benefitting from it' (Pyle, 1980, p. 139).

THE REPLICATION STAGE

In some respects it is correct to describe the replication of a successful pilot, experimental, or demonstration project, strictly as a change in the scale of the operation. The proposal to replicate a small-scale family planning project on a national level, for example, will multiply, to this extent, the need for contraceptive and other supplies. The case-study evidence, however, strongly suggests that the transition to large scale cannot – because it poses problems that differ in kind as well as in degree – normally be successfully effected merely by scaling up the 'ingredients' of the small-scale effort. The evidence to which we are referring emphasizes this important point mainly from two different points of view: political and organizational.

(a) The Political Perspective

Sussman's (1980) study of the fate of Project Etawah, a highly successful community development pilot project in India, describes how 'the change to the national scale raised problems different from those of a project of limited size and duration' (Sussman, 1980, p. 115). In particular, at the very much larger scale the issue shifted from being 'the *best* way of doing community development' to that of 'What is the most politically and bureaucratically *feasible* way to do community development?' (Sussman, 1980, p. 115, emphasis in original). And in this shift of focus the very elements that had made the pilot project a success were lost. For what political expediency appears to have dictated was rapid and wide national coverage and to achieve this with the limited resources at their disposal, the Indian policymakers 'were willing to dilute effective program implementation' by spending fewer resources per unit of operation (effectively sacrificing, in this way, the organizational capacity that had been responsible for the success of the original pilot project).

Pyle's (1981) study of the ill-fated replication of small-scale integrated health, nutrition and family planning projects in Maharashtra, provides further support for the view that the political aspects of the transition to a large scale cannot be extrapolated in any simple way from the small-scale experience. Indeed, he concludes that

> the existing political structure did not obstruct project activities as it did program implementation. Once the project developed model was adopted on a larger scale, political factors became intimately involved in the implementation of the program and had a dramatic effect on the scheme's chances of success.
>
> Pyle, 1981, p. 246

These political difficulties (which, as we shall see below were also closely associated with the organizational failings of the national programme) manifested themselves in a specific set of obstructions, which included the lack of government commitment and elite-group support, the absence of accountability on the part of officials and the discouragement of self-reliance among beneficiary groups.

(b) Organizational Factors

As with the political dimension, small-scale projects generally offer little indication of the exacting organizational problems that are likely to be encountered on a substantially enlarged scale (i.e. at the programme level). The point is that these projects are

> by definition, small in scale and can generally do with simple [organizational] structures. Hence, the structural requirements of replicating a service on a national scale cannot be learnt from their limited experience. *Blowing up the pilot project structure is unlikely to help in most cases.*
>
> Paul, 1982, p. 228, emphasis added

What is required instead, is an organizational structure that is appropriate to the different, more complex problems that emerge at the larger scale and it is on the degree to which this requirement is met that the outcome of replication efforts may very largely depend.

In the attempt to replicate small-scale integrated health, nutrition and population projects in Maharashtra, for example (to which reference has already been made), use of the existing organizational structure to implement the national programme appears to have been highly unsuccessful. The following aspects of this structure, in particular, are thought by Pyle (1981) to have thwarted the replication effort.

(i) Unlike the projects, the procedures adopted at the national level were mostly procedure – rather than results – oriented.

(ii) The governmental operation was characterized by the absence of motivation and 'incentives to promote good morale'.

(iii) Control over the performance of staff was exercised neither by supervision nor effective information systems.

(iv) The highly centralized, hierarchical nature of the health bureaucracy obstructed flexibility in the operation of the program.

(v) Little or no effort was made to foster community interaction.

In so far as these factors can be viewed as a reflection of the attempts by a powerful bureaucracy to resist changes that would threaten its interests, the organizational failings of the large-scale programme become closely allied to its political dimensions that were described above. Pyle himself hints at this interpretation when he notes that 'some officials recognized the need for structural modifications (e.g., effective decentralization, community interaction) ... but adaptations or modifications were resisted by the existing organizational structure' (Pyle, 1981, p. 246). In any event, the problem in this case-study could be described (in the language of organization theory) as a severe mismatch between the existing organizational structure and the new strategy (the term strategy, it should be noted, describes the long-term choice of goals, design of service, policies, and action plans within a programme).[9] Many of the successful cases of replication, in contrast, are distinctive precisely in that they were able to effect a close correspondence between the strategy and structure variables (Korten, 1980; Paul, 1982).

Paul, for example, concludes his study of six such cases with the observation that

In the design and management of development programs, structural interventions are often given inadequate attention. It is not unusual to find innovative and complex strategies being superimposed on weak and rigid structures. The evidence presented ... lends considerable support to the thesis that careful design and dynamic adjustments of structures are important elements in the success of development programs.

Paul, 1982, p. 194

Four lessons, in particular, are suggested in this regard by the case-study material that is reviewed by Paul.

The first is that 'mutual adaptation of program strategies and structures appears to be an essential requirement of success' (Paul, 1982, p. 194). In the successful cases, that is to say, either a relatively rapid adaptation of the organizational structure to the new strategy occurred, or, in circumstances where the former was highly resistant to change, the latter itself was modified. The second lesson is that in large and complex programmes 'network structures' seem to be essential. In these types of structures 'there is no single organization with full control over the program. The national program agency works in coordination with a network of organizations or institutions which jointly provide the components of the program service' (Paul, 1980, p. 118). Since, by definition, the network structure precludes hierarchical control, influence over the institutions in the network is exerted instead by 'lateral' methods (e.g., by joint planning). Third, in contrast to the commonly-held view that beneficiary participation and decentralization are always desirable, the case studies indicate, rather, that the need for these features

is a function of the strategy and environment of a program. That social development programs require more decentralized and participatory structures than conventional economic programs is an important finding. Decentralization and participation are costly.

Paul, 1982, p. 195

Finally, and predictably, the success stories draw attention to the crucial role of organizational autonomy. But this autonomy, it should be emphasized, was not always granted initially to the managers of the programme. Instead, in many cases it was able to be 'induced' by them through various devices (such as working with private firms rather than government agencies). In this way, programme managers were able to forge for themselves a greater degree of autonomy than was nominally conferred on them.

Korten's (1980) review of the five successful Asian cases relates the organizational lessons of this experience to the 'learning process' approach that was discussed earlier in relation to experimental projects. His argument is that it is through this learning process that 'Each project was successful because it had worked out a program model responsive to the beneficiary needs at a particular time and place and each had built a strong organization capable of making the program work' (Korten, 1980, p. 496). He concludes, accordingly, that 'the commonalities that may be looked to as providing important lessons are not found in their final program or organizational blueprints, *but rather in the process by which both program and organization were developed concurrently*' (Korten, 1980, p. 496, emphasis added).

(c) Replication as Commercialization

In part, these bureaucratic and political problems are inherent in the 'public' character of most of the projects referred to above – that is, projects for 'social consumption' where public sector institutions need to be involved. In another category of projects – that which may loosely be described as 'commercial' – the private (rather than the public) sector is able to be the major replication agent. And because many technological innovations are amenable to commercialization, an important role for the private sector in this capacity is envisaged by several authors writing from an appropriate technology perspective.

Jéquier, for example, suggests that

AT groups, despite their substantial investments in research and development, their ability to identify a need for innovation and the originality of the technical solutions they propose, are perhaps not the most adequate institutions to carry out the complex technical work of testing, de-bugging and improving, without which a good prototype cannot be produced successfully on a large scale. This is the sort of work which is carried out extremely effectively by industrial firms, with their research departments, their production engineering teams and their after-sales services.

In this perspective, the growing interest of industrial firms in AT is a phenomenon of major significance: it could, in the long run, help to establish an effective linkage between the industrial production system and the innovative efforts of the AT groups.

Jéquier, 1985, p. 74

This type of collaboration has not, however, been encouraged by the attitude of the appropriate technology institutions, whose egalitarian ideology tends, as Carr (1985) points out, to make them suspicious of the profit motive (especially in relation to large-scale private firms). What is needed, instead, is an approach more like that adopted by the engineering programme of the International Rice Research Institute (IRRI). This programme had as its main objective

to provide local manufacturers technical support and equipment designs with strong commercial potential. The machines were designed to be fabricated using simple, labor intensive techniques, local materials and labor and could be operated and maintained with a minimum of training and mechanical infrastructure. Because of this commercial orientation, IRRI evolved over a period of nearly 10 years, an operational procedure which included assessment of farmer needs and specification of product design parameters followed by design, development, testing and industrial extension.

Duff, 1985, p. 5

In the specific case of the axial flow thresher, Duff (1985) has examined the results of IRRI's commercialization efforts in the Philippines and Thailand. He shows that manufacturers in both countries adopted the new axial flow design extremely rapidly; the result, in his view, of the 'intensive extension effort to demonstrate and promote the design and to provide technical assistance and training to firms cooperating with the program' (Duff, 1985, p. 38).

(d) Replication as 'Institution-Bridging'

Regardless of the type of successful project intervention, replication seems to necessitate a combination of different institutions. This was clearly shown to be the case with the successful replication of projects for 'social consumption' (see under (b) above). Even in the commercialization of the axial flow threshing design by IRRI (described in the previous section) there appeared to be some collaboration with public sector institutions in the countries concerned (Duff, 1985).

And in yet another successful case of replication – that of oral rehydration therapy – a wide variety of institutions (such as multilateral and bilateral foreign aid donors, national public health services and commercial firms) have had a hand in the process (Fricke, 1984).

Conceived in these terms, successful replication often becomes a problem of bringing together and co-ordinating the activities of a diverse set of organizations. David Brown (1987) argues that in these respects 'bridging institutions' can make a significant contribution. Such institutions may in particular be able to forge alliances between constituencies of unequal power ('vertical partnerships') and bring together agencies with relatively equal power, but diverse interests and capacities ('lateral partnerships'). Unfortunately, however,

> Bridging institutions often do not exist. Social scientists and social policy makers alike have paid more attention to organizations at the macro-level (national policy) and at the micro-level (groups, organizations) than to organizational arrangements at the meso-level that link sectors and levels (interorganizational networks and mediating institutions).
>
> Brown, 1987, p. 6

Brown contends that development-oriented private voluntary organizations (DOPVOs) are especially well placed to fill this institutional void, in part because the problems faced by these organizations are inherently similar to those that bridging institutions are likely to confront. As he emphasizes, however, a bridging role will not come easily to all DOPVOs. In particular,

> "First generation," relief-oriented PVOs seldom have the experience with conflicting constituencies or the institution-building skills required. "Second-generation" DOPVOs [oriented to projects] develop capacities for community organizing and project management in creating local projects, and they also have experience with handling constituency conflicts. But such DOPVOs often identify strongly with local clients and remain distant from other institutions (e.g., government agencies) whose long-term involvement is critical to sustaining and replicating the project.... But for DOPVOs that can reconceive development in interinstitutional terms, the potentials for enhanced impact are substantial ... *DOPVOs that engage other agencies and sectors in promoting*

development can potentially produce programs with larger multi-plier effects over time and replication.

Brown, 1987, pp. 17–18, emphasis added

In relation specifically to appropriate technology organizations, this quotation raises several fundamental questions: (a) What degree of departure from their existing modes of operation does a 'reconceived' bridging role imply? (b) What specific changes are needed for these organizations to successfully. implement such a role?

Research on both these questions would seem to be essential for enhancing the replicability of appropriate technology projects.

THE POST-REPLICATION STAGE

As was suggested in Table 4.1, the replication process does not terminate with the implementation of the transition from a small- to a larger-scale operation. For there remains the problem of evaluating the outcome and of using the results of the evaluation to improve future efforts. This post-replication stage has been described as 'One of the most difficult but most important problems in technology transfer' (Doctors, 1969, p. 111). It is important for the obvious reason, that without adequate measurement of results, there is no secure basis on which to judge or improve the existing processes. It is difficult for at least three reasons.

First, as we were concerned to stress in an earlier section, the process by which an innovation spreads is generally a rather slow and unpredictable one. It is accordingly difficult to know exactly when the results of the process ought to be measured. Second, when an innovation is transferred on a commercial basis, adopters may be reluctant, for competitive reasons, to divulge its source. Precisely this problem appears, for example, to have made it difficult to obtain evidence of the industrial usage of NASA technology (Doctors, 1969). Third, an innovation may undergo various 'mutations' during the adoption process. Rogers (1983) refers to this phenomenon as 're-invention' and notes that

Until very recently we assumed that adoption of an innovation meant the exact copying or imitation of how the innovation had been used previously in a different setting. Sometimes the adoption of an innovation does indeed represent identical behaviour. . . . In many other cases, however, an innovation is not invariant as it diffuses.

Rogers, 1983, p. 175

C. Weiss *et al.* (1982) distinguish between two different types of 're-invention'.

> One can be called 'adaptation of component features' of an innovation. Instead of adopting the new technology intact, people may select certain components of the innovation and use them in other settings and for other purposes.... A second type of diffusion can be called 'diffusion to new uses'. In these cases, the specific product ... is used for purposes other than those for which it was originally intended.
>
> Weiss *et al.*, 1982, pp. 1–2

Perhaps because of these and other difficulties, the measurement problem has received comparatively little attention in the literature (Weiss, *et al.*, 1982). In a recent survey of what material on the subject is available, Weiss *et al.*, (1982) propose a methodology that is based on first identifying the spread of an innovation and then measuring its intensity. For the former purpose, the following seven techniques are advocated: physical tracers (an ideal-type method that is based on the medical practice of using radioactive tracers); communication trails (the idea of 'charting the trail' of people who were involved with the innovation at the original project site); attendance at demonstrations and fairs (learning about the innovation by visiting the original demonstration site and other places where the innovation is promoted); informants and snowball samples (using informants to name others, produces, ultimately, a snowball effect); parallel organizations (e.g. in cases where the innovation is an institutional arrangement, one can profitably search for other, parallel institutions); back-tracing from chance observations (using a chance observation to inquire from the user where information about the innovation originated); theory and speculation (using theoretical principles and informed guesses).

Once one or more of these techniques – which differ in terms of their efficacy, time, costs and required expertise – have been used to identify the location of any spread effects, the intensity or size of these effects have then to be measured. For this purpose, as Weiss *et al.* (1982) discovered from their extensive review of the literature, six alternative methods seem to be available, namely, sample surveys, informant interviewing, ethnography, records/documents, observation/visual inspection, and aggregate statistics. Here again, these authors emphasize that because they possess different advantages and disadvantages (e.g. cost, validity, precision, etc.), the alternatives are appropriate to varying circumstances.

As an illustration of some of the points raised in this section, it is useful to consider a specific example, and for this purpose we have selected the case of the axial flow thresher. This innovation, as noted, was developed and promoted by the International Rice Research Institute in the Philippines, and recently Duff (1985) has attempted to evaluate the rate of return to the expenditures on the project. His calculations illustrate several of the issues involved in the *ex-post* evaluation of replication efforts.

It turns out, for example, that the cost-benefit ratio is sensitive to the period over which it is estimated: indeed, only after the first ten years (when an intensive extension effort was undertaken) did this ratio become positive. Duff also had to confront the problem of tracing the spread of the axial threshers and of estimating the extent of this effect. For the solution to the former, he appears to have relied mostly on the 'parallel organization' method. That is, he sought to identify the location of spread effects by focusing not on the ultimate users of the new threshers, but on the manufacturers of these products instead: in particular, those manufacturers who participated in the IRRI Extension Programme. Moreover, by using what 'reasonable statistics' were available on the annual sales of threshers he was able also to measure the extent of spread (though, as he acknowledges, this procedure leads to an underestimate in so far as it neglects 'the large numbers of firms who are not formally associated with the IRRI project but which have freely copied the design from participating firms').[10]

SUMMARY AND CONCLUSIONS

The main findings of this review may be summarized in terms of the following propositions.

1. Except in some rather unusual circumstances, replication has to concern itself with more stages of the project cycle than only that which deals with the diffusion of an innovation.

2. Because it for the most part ignores these other stages, traditional diffusion research throws only limited light on the more complex problem of replication.

3. At each stage in this more complex process, the implications for replication need to be drawn from a wide variety of different literatures, spanning a range of disciplines.

4. The lessons to be drawn from these diverse sources have mostly to do with overcoming the fundamental problem of uncertainty that inheres with varying degrees of severity at the different stages, and which has both a supply- and demand-side dimension.

5. From the discussion of the initial, design and selection stage, the conclusion was drawn that the purpose of replication ought not to be viewed as the wide dissemination of an innovation *per se*. It is almost always possible to raise the probability that an innovation will be adopted by increasing the amount that is spent on extension/diffusion. The objective, rather, is to achieve widespread diffusion at relatively low cost, or more generally, to seek to raise the benefits from replication in relation to the costs. This ratio will tend to be most favourable in circumstances that give rise to the rapid diffusion, at low cost, of an innovation, that is highly productive, has significant macroeconomic implications and a high probability of adoption. Much of the first part of the chapter was concerned with identifying the factors that are likely to be conducive to these favourable circumstances. For this purpose, a number of simple techniques were described, including a simplified version of the farming systems research method.

6. Even if these various procedures are adopted, however, a considerable degree of uncertainty will normally still attend the projects that are selected and for this reason, they will need to be introduced on an initially small scale.

7. At this stage of the project cycle, it is essential to recognize that there are different types of small-scale projects, serving different purposes and containing correspondingly different mechanisms through which the probability of replication may be enhanced. In particular, pilot projects were seen to operate through an evaluative mode, experimental projects through a process of learning, and demonstration projects via mainly the support and persuasion that they are able to engender.

8. The transition from one or more of these types of small-scale projects to a much larger scale of operations (i.e. the replication

stage proper), can only partly be described as a process in which all relevant elements are simply 'scaled-up' to a proportionate extent. For many of the most intractable difficulties of the transition (especially those of a political and organizational nature) seem to arise precisely because of, and are peculiar to, the enlargement of the scale of the operation (and which cannot, therefore, be observed at the scale of the smaller projects described above).

9. If appropriate technology organizations are to play a significant role in enhancing the replicability of small-scale projects, they will need to pay more attention to collaboration possibilities with the private sector (via 'commercialization') and with other replication agents (via 'institution-bridging').

10. As we conceive of it, the replication process does not terminate with the attempted transition from a small to a larger scale. What remains is the difficult task of evaluating the outcome of this effort, a task that is frequently made the more difficult by the 'mutations' that an innovation undergoes in the process of spread itself.

5 Conclusions

Even with a quite rapid rate of growth of the modern sector, many developing countries will face the problem of increasing numbers living outside this sector for the next thirty to forty years. And by the time these numbers cease to grow in absolute terms, the non-modern sector will have become a multiple of its present size. These projections are alarming, among other reasons, because they suggest that unprecedented numbers will become reliant upon traditional (usually unproductive) rural technologies. The previous chapters have dealt with different aspects of alleviating this growing problem by improving the productivity of traditional rural technologies. Chapter 1 was concerned with the alternative frames of reference in the improvement of these technologies. Chapter 2 examined the relationship between the diffusion of improved technologies and the rate of their adoption within the scope of a particular project. In Chapter 3 there was a discussion of the economic relationships that link the adoption of improved technology to the supposed beneficiaries among the poor. Chapter 4 took up the problem of seeking the replication on a large scale of projects that prove successful at the micro level.

It is useful for policy purposes to classify the major findings of these chapters into three different levels of analysis, namely, micro, meso and macro. A classification along these lines is helpful in delineating the areas of responsibility for policy changes and hence also in assessing the feasibility of such changes.

THE MICRO LEVEL

Improvement of traditional technologies and diffusion of these innovations to project-level beneficiaries are the primary concerns of many appropriate technology organizations. Our review of the former topic in Chapter 1 showed that efforts to improve traditional rural technologies may take the form of upgrading these technologies, descaling modern alternatives or of replacement investment. Upgrading carries the implication that there are intrinsically worthwhile elements of the traditional technology which need to be retained in the process of creating an improved alternative. The descaling strategy, in contrast, has as its frame of reference the technological shelf developed in and for the advanced countries. It is by the descaling of these modern technologies to the village level that this approach seeks to raise the productivity of producers who formerly were reliant on traditional methods. According to the third approach – that of replacement investment – the existing base of scientific and technical knowledge is applied directly to generating an alternative technology, which, as with descaling, replaces rather than builds upon the elements of traditional technologies. Although we found some (apparently successful) examples in each category, it is impossible to fully assess the scope of each. In the case of upgrading, for example, the difficulty arises partly because the potential afforded by this approach tends to be systematically undervalued by the formal R&D system. With respect to descaling, it is difficult to assess the emerging potential that is associated with the miniaturization possibilities of microelectronics. Much of the scope of descaling, moreover, was seen to depend on a variety of institutional factors, the prevalence of which in different parts of the Third World is difficult to establish.

The diffusion of improved technologies to project-level beneficiaries, as noted, is the second major component of the appropriate technology approach. Chapter 2 comprises an analysis of project case-study material with the objective of isolating the main factors that account for the instances of success as well as of failure in the diffusion and adoption of improved technologies (with particular emphasis on those that are upgraded). One of the conclusions that emerges from a study of this material is that the choice of a suitable approach to diffusion needs to reflect the variation in the nature of the technology that is to be improved. In particular, distinctions need to be drawn between technologies for production and those for consumption; technologies that can be diffused on an individualistic basis as opposed to those that require some communal form of organization; and technologies that are located 'on the farm' in rural areas and those that are associated with non-farm activities. A second major conclusion of this chapter is that whatever the particular combination of these characteristics that an improved technology comprises, it is the ability to determine the user requirements with which they are associated, that primarily determines the success or failure of dissemination efforts. Farming systems research offers a promising methodology for understanding the technological needs of small farmers but the exponents of this method have tended to ignore the many problems of its implementation. They have also (as suggested in Chapter 4) generally neglected to assess the research costs of the method in relation to its incremental benefits measured by higher adoption rates (that is, the efficiency of farming systems research has not been adequately investigated).

Chapters 3 and 4 are both critical of an approach that would include *only* the issues raised so far in this section; that is, an approach that is based on making improved technologies available to the target group of poor living outside the modern sector. These two chapters are concerned, therefore, to propose a broader framework than is normally associated with the appropriate technology movement and they suggest on this basis that there is much more that can be done at the micro level to enhance the impact of improved technologies on rural poverty.

The main purpose of Chapter 3 is to question the view that adoption of improved technologies should be regarded as the ultimate desideratum of policy: a sufficient condition of a successful project outcome. It contends that this view neglects an important set of variables which considerably complicate the impact of adoption on the target group of poor. When these variables are included in the analysis, it is found that adoption of improved technologies may or may not help to alleviate poverty and reduce inequality.

Much was shown to depend on the differential impact of improved technology on the heterogeneous groups (such as the unemployed, the working poor, small farmers) living in poverty. In some cases, apparently appropriate new technologies may leave unchanged or even worsen the economic standing of the groups that comprise the majority of the poor. In other cases, where it turns out to be well matched with the specific composition of the poor in a particular country, technological change will have a far more favourable distributional impact. Much was also shown to depend on the extent to which the benefits that are potentially available to the adopter(s) of an innovation are actually realized. Numerous examples attest to the facts that new technologies may be used inefficiently, may be poorly maintained or even discontinued altogether. What data are available suggest that these problems can be avoided or reduced if a high degree of involvement of local users is elicited in the design and implementation of the new technology (a conclusion similar to that reached in Chapter 2). The final variable that appears to strongly influence the outcome of improved technologies is the nature of the relationship over time between the non-modern and modern sectors.

Where this relationship is competitive (rather than complementary or non-existent) traditional producers compete over time with the products of the technologically dynamic modern sector (or with imports). Improved technologies must then be judged against this intertemporal criterion as well as their immediate impact on the incomes of traditional producers and consumers. Clearly, the long-term condition will be met by neither a merely once-for-all improvement nor by one whose viability over time depends on continual government subsidization.

Chapter 4 deals with the requirements for successful replication of interventions at the micro level. Though widespread replication is now being sought by some AT advocates, there is in fact little in the methodology of the AT approach that will systematically contribute to this outcome. In particular, with its emphasis on the engineering problems of improving traditional technologies and on the diffusion of these improvements to project beneficiaries, the AT approach lacks a micro procedure for selecting and designing projects so as to raise the probability of their ultimate replication. Chapter 4 advocates a framework in which these neglected issues are dealt with in the general context of decision-making under uncertainty. There will be more on this below.

Some of the major concerns expressed in Chapters 3 and 4 (and summarized in the foregoing paragraphs) need to be systematized in a revised AT methodology.[1] There is a need, first to incorporate *ex ante* the distributional implications of improved rural technologies. The starting point of such efforts should be identification of the composition of the target poor in each case. Then, using simple partial equilibrium tools it is sometimes possible to arrive at the approximate distributional effects of the technical change on these poverty groups. In other cases, a more complex intersectoral analysis will be required to estimate these effects. Whichever form of economic analysis is used, however, some attempt needs to be made (*ex-ante* as well as *ex-post*) to fill in the cells of a matrix such as Table 3.2 above.

There is a need also to systematize replication concerns in *ex ante* project analysis. The stage of screening and selecting projects is one in which scarce resources have to be allocated among projects whose ultimate potential for replicability at this early point in the project cycle is especially uncertain. In order to deal effectively with this initially acute uncertainty, and thus to allocate resources to the projects with the highest probabilities of being replicated, it was found to be useful to employ the framework of *ex ante* cost-benefit analysis. Use of this framework (which has often been employed in problems of research resource allocation in agriculture) suggests that the purpose of replication ought not to be viewed as the wide dissemination of an innovation *per se*. The objective, rather, should be that of achieving widespread diffusion at relatively low cost, or more generally, to seek to raise the benefits from replication in relation to the costs. This objective is unlikely to be realized by the use of techniques (such as farming systems research) that require very high research costs. What are required instead are simple techniques that raise the probability of widespread adoption of new technologies *without* a significant increase in the costs of research. Various techniques described in Chapter 4 (such as environmental sensitivity and replicability indices and a simplified version of farming systems research) appear to satisfy this requirement partly because their methodological simplicity encourages the type of interaction among disciplines that is required for the efficient allocation of research resources.

Even if the techniques described in the previous paragraph are adopted, however, a considerable degree of uncertainty will normally still attend the projects that are selected and for this reason they will need to be introduced on an initially small (and inexpensive) scale. At this stage of the project cycle it is essential to recognize that there are different types of small-scale projects, serving different purposes and containing correspondingly different mechanisms through which the probability of replication may be enhanced. In particular, pilot projects operate according to the evaluative principles of the scientific method, experimental projects operate through a process of learning and demonstration projects via the support and persuasion that they are able to engender. An important question is then raised as to whether AT projects should properly be considered as experimental, demonstration, or pilot projects; or, more precisely, *which* types of AT projects fall into *which* categories. And once this is established, further questions concern the specific manner in which AT organizations ought to promote replication in each case. How, for example, might a 'learning process approach' based on experimental projects be implemented? How exactly should AT organizations engage in 'public relations' and the 'selling' of new approaches exhibited through demonstration projects? How should the location for these types of projects be selected? Finally, what degree of departure from existing practice is implied by the answers to these questions?

THE MESO LEVEL

The transition from one or more of these types of small-scale project to a much larger scale of operations (that is, the replication stage proper) may be regarded as falling into the meso-level category of interventions (those that are intermediate between the micro and macro levels). Some of the conclusions drawn at this level of analysis are applicable mostly to the public sector, which, in the case of projects for social consumption, is normally the main agent of replication. A review of (mostly) these types of projects (in Chapter 4) showed, for example, that replication can only partly be described as a process in which all relevant elements are simply 'scaled-up' to a proportionate extent. The reason is that many of the most intractable problems of the transition – especially those of a political and organizational nature – seem to arise precisely because of, and are peculiar to, the enlargement of the scale of the operation. Because these difficulties necessarily cannot be observed at the scale of the smaller projects described above, careful consideration needs to be given to the form that they are likely to take in each case.[2]

There also are lessons at the meso level for AT organizations. If these organizations are to play a significant role in enhancing the replicability of small-scale projects, they will need to pay far more attention to collaboration possibilities with the private sector (via 'commercialization') and with other replication agents (via 'institution bridging'). It is worth emphasizing that *both* of these functions will often be needed because even 'commercial' projects (which have the private sector as the major replication agent) seem to require collaboration among different institutions.

THE MACRO LEVEL

It was argued in Chapter 3 that the viability of improved rural technologies is a function not merely of the immediate competitive relationships confronting these technologies, but also of the conditions that determine whether a vibrant small-scale capital goods sector comes into being. Both of these determinants of viability were shown to be heavily influenced by government policies (with respect, for example, to prices and product standards). The form of these policies, in turn, depends to a large degree on the overall rural development strategy that is pursued. Where a 'bimodal' strategy is followed (that is, one based on a highly dualistic size structure of farm and non-farm units), policies and resources are geared to the dominance of large-scale units and the ensuing economic environment appears to 'choke off' the evolution of the process of improving traditional technologies. Where, in contrast, a 'unimodal' strategy – emphasizing the progressive modernization of the entire rural sector – is pursued, the macro-environment is much more favourable to the long-term viability of improvements in traditional technology. It is doubtless at least partly for this reason that whereas many of the successful cases in our study were found in India (which has followed a bimodal pattern), numerous of the successful outcomes were drawn from Taiwan and China (both of which are examples of the workings of a unimodal pattern).

These findings ought to be viewed as forming part of a growing awareness of the importance of government policies for the success or failure of AT. A recent volume edited by Frances Stewart (1987) contains considerable case-study evidence on this question. Much of the evidence suggests that government policies in the Third World tend to promote inappropriate rather than appropriate technologies and that altering the direction of these policies would encounter substantial political opposition (from those who would stand to lose in the process).[3] This political economy dimension raises an important possibility: on the one hand, because they are inherently so pervasive, changes in macro policy are likely to have a more significant impact on efforts to improve traditional technologies than changes at the micro or meso levels.[4] On the other hand, however, changes at these lower levels of intervention (including those that we have advocated) may be easier to implement, precisely because they tend to impinge on a narrower range of political interests. Much depends, however, on the particular form that the interventions take at each level: whether, for example, they pose a direct threat to the interest groups associated with inappropriate technologies, or whether they give positive support to AT without at the same time challenging these vested interests.[5]

Notes

CHAPTER 1: INTRODUCTION

1. In the introduction to the chapter on intermediate technology he makes it clear that his concern is solely that of 'helping the people in the non-modern sector' (Schumacher, 1973, p. 143).
2. See Jéquier and Blanc (1983).
3. In its 1986 Workplan, Appropriate Technology International formulated a replication strategy. This proposed 'the dissemination or diffusion of the innovative element(s) of a successful appropriate technology project of ATI beyond the objectives and implementation plan of the original project' (ATI, 1986, p. 9).
4. See, for example, Stewart (1987).
5. See, for example, Stewart (1977) and Johnston and Clark (1982).
6. See Oberai (1978).
7. See IBRD (1978).
8. See IBRD (1978).
9. These are defined by Forsyth, McBain and Solomon (1982).
10. See Wong (1982).
11. See Wong (1982).
12. See Kaplinsky (1987), Rosenberg (1986) and Bhalla *et al.* (1984).
13. See Garg (1976).

CHAPTER 2: DIFFUSION AND ADOPTION

1. See Johnston and Kilby (1975).
2. See Macpherson and Jackson (1975, p.118).
3. See Kaplinsky (1983).
4. See IBRD (1978).
5. Quoted in Johnston and Kilby (1975, p. 354).
6. See Johnston and Kilby (1975).
7. See Johnston and Kilby (1975).
8. See Barwell and Howe (1979).
9. See Moulik and Purushotham (1983).
10. It should be noted that in some countries such as Indonesia, Kenya, Mali, Nigeria and Thailand women have also been principal food producers See IBRD (1985).
11. See Agarwal (1983).
12. See Soedjarwo (1981).
13. For a discussion see Freire (1968).
14. See Olson (1965).
15. See Kalbermatten *et al.* (1980).
16. See Coward (1977).

17. See Moulik and Purushotham (1983).
18. See, for example, Collinson (1982).
19. See Chambers and Ghildyal (1985).
20. See Chambers and Ghildyal (1985).

CHAPTER 3: THE IMPACT OF ADOPTION ON THE POOR

1. See, for example, Behrman (1979).
2. Greeley's (1982) study of rice processing in Bangladesh shows that labour-saving techniques 'are spreading because they reduce costs . . . and the labour displaced, from the poorest households, is usually female' (Greeley, 1982, p. 20). He argues that if the benefits from this type of technical change are to reach female wage labourers and their families 'carefully planned cooperative approaches to changing ownership patterns' are required (Greeley, 1982, p. 21).
3. See Duff (1985).
4. See Binswanger (1980).
5. See Duff (1985).
6. See Duff (1985).
7. See Griffin and James (1981).
8. See Agarwal (1983).
9. See Fricke (1984).
10. See Zeidenstein (1980).
11. See Darrow *et al.* (1981).
12. See, for example, Watanabe (1983).
13. See Page (1979).
14. For the Korean and Taiwanese cases see Ho (1980).
15. See Stewart (1977).
16. See Spence (1978).

CHAPTER 4: THE REPLICABILITY OF DEVELOPMENT PROJECTS

1. The 'replicability index' developed by Morss *et al.* (1975), is an example of how this problem might be tackled in practice. The index reflects (on a scale of 1 to 5) the applicability (in the eyes of those who are closely involved) of each project to many different locations and environments.

    This index was intended to reveal such unusual project features as the social and cultural solidarity of the Tiv people in Nigeria. . . . The index also singled out leadership requirements imposed by the highly developed and sophisticated organizational structure of the OESEC project in Bolivia. It is unlikely that ordinary men could initiate and manage the same kind of development program in another environment.

    Morss *et al.*, 1975, p. 260

2. Some indirect light, however, is thrown on this empirical question by Kottak's (1985) results. On the basis of a review of 68 World Bank projects, he shows that the average rate of return for rural development projects that were regarded as incorporating a sociological analysis, was considerably higher than that for projects which did not embody such an analysis. His methodology does not make it clear, though, whether these differential rates of return are due to variations in rates of adoption or to some other factors.

3. The point is also emphasized by Bagadion and Korten (1985).

4. See Norman (1978).

5. In their discussion of the replicability of shelter projects, Baum and Tolbert (1985) draw attention to the scarcity of available land in reasonable proximity to employment opportunities. This means that as the program expands

> project sites may entail higher land costs; or they may be farther from employment opportunities, in which case the attractiveness of the project to low-income groups is reduced unless additional investments are made to improve transportation to the project site or to generate employment opportunities nearby.
>
> Baum and Tolbert, 1985, p. 298

6. A similar conclusion was also reached much earlier by Hirschman, who, in 1967, observed that 'Some of the most successful projects we have come across are those that have experienced substantial uncertainties and difficulties' (Hirschman, 1967, p. 85). Most recently, this argument has been stated by Biggs (1984) in relation to the highly successful Grameen Bank Project in Bangladesh. The Bank was established in 1982 with funds from the Bangladesh Bank and the International Fund for Agricultural Development (*The Economist*, 18 October 1986). It has subsequently grown to a size where it assists 250 000 borrowers drawn from among the poorest classes in Bangladesh. In seeking to explain this outcome Biggs (1984, p. 67) finds it significant that the project 'evolved cautiously out of a locally conceived and locally initiated action research project'. Though, as he points out, there were problems from the outset, the issues 'were addressed and solutions were found as the project progressed. . . . The result was that a scheme evolved which worked successfully when replicated elsewhere' (p. 68). Biggs concludes that

> the Grameen Bank Project illustrates how action research, when carried out within local institutional structures, can produce feasible solutions. Action research, when carried out under "special project" conditions may not produce solutions for widespread diffusion.
>
> Biggs, 1984, p. 69

7. In this regard, Hirschman suggests that there are many areas 'where the habit of deciding in advance in favor of the *one best way* can be advantageously replaced by a more experimental approach allowing

for some sequential decision making' (Hirschman, 1967, p. 82, emphasis in original). He points, for example, to coping with the uncertainty about the 'direction in which road traffic and new settlements will develop', by building several cheap roads instead of a single expensive one and waiting 'for cues from the ensuing traffic to decide which one should be improved and perhaps paved' (Hirschman, 1967, p. 83).

8. Rondinelli (1983).
9. Paul (1982).
10. Duff (1985, pp. 29–30).

CHAPTER 5: CONCLUSIONS

1. The systematization that is advocated below is similar in emphasis to Binswanger and Ryan's (1977) discussion of the *ex-ante* allocation of research resources.
2. Pyle (1981, p. 266) suggests the need for 'an exercise which might be referred to as a Pre-Program Potential Impact Evaluation'. Because this exercise would include sociopolitical constraints it 'goes beyond the normal feasibility study which has traditionally been primarily economic in nature' (Pyle, 1981, p. 266).
3. It is for much the same reason that the outcome of government efforts to improve traditional technologies often diverges from the appearance of enthusiasm with which they are pursued. In the case of India, for example, partly because of the

> conflicting pulls and pushes of interest groups, implementation of various policy measures favouring decentralized rural industries has been tardy, half-hearted, and at best counterproductive.
> Moulik and Purushotham, 1983, p. 15

Tanzania's failure to promote the widespread use of animal-drawn implements is especially noteworthy, for

> it might be assumed that as a socialist country with a strong commitment to an egalitarian approach to development, the political pressures which have elsewhere contributed to the encouragement of inappropriately capital-intensive technologies would have been almost nonexistent. However, the gap between policy pronouncements and actual implementation has been wide.
> Johnston, 1981, p. 21

4. Stewart (1987).
5. This distinction is made by Stewart (1987).

References

B. Agarwal, 'Diffusion of Rural Innovations: Some Analytical Issues and the Case of Wood-burning Stoves', *World Development*, vol. 11(4), 1983.

I. Ahmed and B. Kinsey (eds), *Farm Equipment Innovations in Eastern and Central Southern Africa*, Gower, 1984.

Appropriate Technology International, '1986 Annual Workplan', Washington, D.C., 1986.

A. Bachmann and A. Nakarmi, *New Himalayan Water Wheels*, Sahayogi Press, Kathmandu, 1983.

B. Bagadion and F. Korten, 'Developing Irrigators Organizations: a Learning Process Approach' in M. Cernea (ed.), *Putting People First*, Oxford University Press, 1985.

I. Barwell and J. Howe, 'Appropriate Transport Facilities for the Rural Sector in Developing Countries' in UNIDO, *Appropriate Industrial Technology for Low-Cost Transport for Rural Areas*, Monographs on Appropriate Industrial Technology, no 2, UNIDO, 1979.

W. Baum and S. Tolbert, *Investing in Development: Lessons of World Bank Experience*, Oxford University Press, 1985.

J. R. Behrman, 'International Commodity Agreements: An Evaluation of the UNCTAD Integrated Commodity Programme' in W. R. Cline (ed.), *Policy Alternatives for a New International Economic Order*, Praeger, 1979.

A. S. Bhalla, D. James and Y. Stevens, *Blending of New and Traditional Technologies*, Tycooly, 1984.

S. Biggs, 'Awkward but Common Themes in Agricultural Policy' in E. J. Clay and B. B. Schaffer (eds), *Room for Manoeuvre: an Exploration of Public Policy in Agriculture and Rural Development*, Heinemann, 1984.

S. Biggs, and E. Clay, 'Generation and Diffusion of Agricultural Technology: a Review of Theories and Experiences', ILO, World Employment Programme, Working Paper, no. 122, 1983.

H. Binswanger, 'Income Distribution Effects of Technical Change: Some Analytical Issues', *South East Asian Economic Review*, vol. 1(3), December 1980.

H. Binswanger, 'Agricultural Mechanization: a Comparative Historical Perspective', Research Unit, Agriculture and Rural Development Department, World Bank, 1982.

H. Binswanger and J. Ryan, 'Efficiency and Equity Issues in *Ex Ante* Allocation of Research Resources', *Indian Journal of Agricultural Economics*, vol. 32(3), 1977.

H. Binswanger and V. Ruttan, *Induced Innovation*, Johns Hopkins University Press, 1978.

N. Birdsall, 'Population Growth and the Structural Transformation of the Labor Force', Paper for Presentation at Annual Meetings of the Population Association of America, Boston, 28–30 Mar. 1985.

E. Boserup, *Population and Technological Change*, University of Chicago Press, 1982.

127

V. Brandt and J. Cheong, 'Planning from the Bottom Up: Community-Based Integrated Rural Development in South Korea' in P. Coombs (ed.), *Meeting the Basic Needs of the Rural Poor*, Pergamon, 1980.

L. David Brown, 'Private Voluntary Organizations and Development Partnerships', Paper Prepared for the Conference on Organizational and Behavioral Perspectives for Social Development, Indian Institute of Management, Ahmedabad, India, 29 Dec. 1986 to 2 Jan. 1987.

D. Byerlee, L. Harrington and D. Winkelman, 'Farming Systems Research: Issues in Research Strategy and Technology Design', *American Journal of Agricultural Economics*, vol. 64(5), Dec. 1982.

M. Carr, *The AT Reader: Theory and Practice in Appropriate Technology*, Intermediate Technology Publications, 1985.

R. Chambers, 'Project Selection for Poverty Focused Rural Development: Simple is Optimal', *World Development*, vol. 6(2), Feb. 1978.

R. Chambers and B. P. Ghildyal, 'Agricultural Research for Resource – Poor Farmers: the Farmer-First-and-Last Model', IDS Sussex, Discussion Paper 203, Apr. 1985.

F. C. Child and H. Kaneda, 'Links to the Green Revolution: a Study of Small-Scale, Agriculturally Related Industry in the Pakistan Punjab', *Economic Development and Cultural Change*, vol. 23(2), Jan. 1975.

M. Collinson, 'Farming Systems Research in Eastern Africa: the Experience of CIMMYT and Some National Agricultural Research Services, 1976–1981', Michigan State University International Development Paper, no. 3, 1982.

P. Coombs and M. Ahmed, *Attacking Rural Poverty*, Johns Hopkins University Press, 1974.

E. Walter Coward, 'Irrigation Management Alternatives: Themes from Indigenous Irrigation Systems', *Agricultural Administration*, 4, 1977.

R. Cuca and C. Pierce, *Experiments in Family Planning: Lessons from the Developing World*, Johns Hopkins University Press, 1977.

K. Darrow *et al.*, *Appropriate Technology Sourcebook*, vol. 2, Volunteers in Asia Publication, 1981.

S. Doctors, *The Role of Federal Agencies in Technology Transfer*, MIT Press, 1969.

B. Duff, 'Changes in Small Farm Paddy Threshing Technology in Thailand and the Philippines', Appropriate Technology International, Washington D.C., 1985.

K. Easter and G. Norton, 'Potential Returns from Increased Research for the Land Grant Universities', *Agricultural Economics Research*, vol. 29(4), Oct., 1977.

M. Elmendorf and P. Buckles, *Appropriate Technology for Water Supply and Sanitation: Sociocultural Aspects of Water Supply and Excreta Disposal*, World Bank, Dec. 1980.

G. Fairweather and L. Tornatzky, *Experimental Methods for Social Policy Research*, Pergamon, 1977.

G. Feder, R. Just and D. Zilberman, 'Adoption of Agricultural Innovations in Developing Countries', World Bank Staff Working Paper, no. 542, 1982.

C. Frank and R. Webb (eds), *Income Distribution and Growth in the Less Developed Countries*, Brookings, 1977.

P. Francks, 'The Development of New Techniques in Agriculture: the Case of the Mechanization of Irrigation in the Saga Plain Area of Japan', *World Development*, vol. 7(4/5), Apr./May 1979.

P. Freire, *Pedagogy of the Oppressed*, Seabury Press, 1968.

T. Fricke, 'High Impact Appropriate Technology Case Studies', Appropriate Technology International, Washington, D.C., 1984.

D. Forsyth, N. McBain and R. Solomon, 'Technical Rigidity and Appropriate Technology in Less Developed Countries' in F. Stewart and J. James (eds), *The Economics of New Technology in Developing Countries*, Frances Pinter, 1982.

M. K. Garg, 'The Scaling-Down of Modern Technology: Crystal Sugar Manufacturing in India' in N. Jéquier (ed.), *Appropriate Technology: Problems and Promises*, OECD, 1976.

M. Gillis *et al.*, *Economic Development*, Norton, 1983.

M. Greeley, 'Rural Technology, Rural Institutions and the Rural Poorest: the Case of Rice Processing in Bangladesh', IDS, Sussex, Discussion Paper 154, Nov. 1982.

K. Griffin and J. James, *The Transition to Egalitarian Development*, Macmillan, 1981.

J. Guiltinan and G. Paul, *Marketing Management*, 2nd edn, McGraw-Hill, 1985.

D. Hapgood, *Policies for Promoting Agricultural Development*, MIT Center for International Studies, 1965.

Y. Hayami, *A Century of Agricultural Growth in Japan*, University of Minnesota Press, 1975.

E. Heinemann and S. Biggs, 'Farming Systems Research: an Evolutionary Approach to Implementation', *Journal of Agricultural Economics*, vol. XXXVI(1), Jan. 1985.

A. Hirschman, *Development Projects Observed*, Brookings, 1967.

S. Ho, 'Small-Scale Enterprises in Korea and Taiwan', World Bank Staff Working Paper, no. 384, 1980.

M. Howes, 'The Social and Economic Implications of Alternative Approaches to Small Scale Irrigation in Bangladesh', IDS, Sussex, mimeo, n.d.

M. Howes and R. Chambers, 'Indigenous Technical Knowledge: Analysis, Implications and Issues' in D. Brokensha, D. Warren and O. Werner (eds), *Indigenous Knowledge Systems and Development*, University Press of America, 1980.

IBRD, *Rural Enterprise and Nonfarm Employment*, Washington, D.C., 1978.

IBRD, *Agricultural Research and Extension*, Washington, D.C., 1985.

D. Ironmonger, *New Commodities and Consumer Behaviour*, Cambridge University Press, 1972.

S. Ishikawa, *Essays on Technology, Employment and Institutions in Economic Development*, Economic Research Series, Hitotsubashi University, 1981.

M. A. Jabbar, 'Commercialization of Agricultural Equipment Generated by R&D System in Bangladesh', ILO, World Employment Programme, Working Paper, no. 155, Sept. 1985.

N. Jéquier, (ed.), *Appropriate Technology: Problems and Promises*, OECD, 1976.

N. Jéquier, 'Appropriate Technology – Ten Years On' in M. Carr (ed.) *The AT Reader: Theory and Practice in Appropriate Technology*, Intermediate Technology Publications, 1985.

N. Jéquier and G. Blanc, *The World of Appropriate Technology*, OECD, 1983.

B. Johnston, 'Farm Equipment Innovations and Rural Industrialisation in Eastern Africa: an Overview', ILO, World Employment Programme, Working Paper, no. 80, 1981.

B. Johnston, 'Farm Equipment Innovations in Eastern Africa: Policy Considerations' in I. Ahmed and B. Kinsey (eds), *Farm Equipment Innovations in Eastern and Central Southern Africa*, Gower, 1984.

B. Johnston and W. Clark, *Redesigning Rural Development*, Johns Hopkins University Press, 1982.

B. Johnston and P. Kilby, *Agriculture and Structural Transformation*, Oxford University Press, 1975.

J. Kalbermatten *et al.*, *Appropriate Technology for Water Supply and Sanitation: a Summary of Technical and Economic Options*, World Bank, 1980.

R. Kaplinsky, *Sugar Processing: the Development of a Third-World Technology*, Intermediate Technology Publications, 1983.

R. Kaplinsky, *Micro-electronics and Employment Revisited*, ILO, World Employment Programme, 1987.

D. Korten, 'Community Organization and Rural Development: a Learning Process Approach', *Public Administration Review*, Sept./Oct. 1980.

C. Kottak, 'When People Don't Come First: Some Sociological Lessons from Completed Projects' in M. Cernea (ed.), *Putting People First*, Oxford University Press, 1985.

W. Arthur Lewis, 'The Dual Economy Revisited', *The Manchester School*, vol. XLVII(3), Sept. 1979.

G. MacPherson and D. Jackson, 'Village Technology for Rural Development', *International Labour Review*, Feb. 1975.

S. Maxwell, 'The Social Scientist in Farming Systems Research', IDS, Sussex, Discussion Paper 199, Nov. 1984.

D. Morgan and D. Mara, *Ventilated Pit Latrines: Recent Developments in Zimbabwe*, World Bank Technical Paper no. 3, 1982.

E. Morss *et al.*, *Strategies for Small Farmer Development*, vol. 1, Westview, 1975.

T. K. Moulik and P. Purushotham, *Technology Transfer Process in Decentralized Rural Industries*, Indian Institute of Management, Ahmedabad, 1983.

D. Norman, 'Farming Systems Research to Improve the Livelihood of Small Farmers', *American Journal of Agricultural Economics*, vol. 60(5), Dec. 1978.

A. S. Oberai, *Changes in the Structure of Employment with Economic Development*, ILO, 1978.

M. S. Olson Jr, *The Logic of Collective Action*, Harvard University Press, 1965.

J. Page, 'Small Enterprises in African Development: a Survey', World Bank Staff Working Paper, no. 363, 1979.

A. Pacey, *Hand-Pump Maintenance*, Intermediate Technology Development Group, 1977. Quoted in K. Darrow *et al.*, *Appropriate Technology Sourcebook*, vol. 2, Volunteers in Asia Publications, 1981.

S. Paul, *Managing Development Programs*, Westview, 1982.

D. Perkins *et al.*, *Rural Small-Scale Industry in the People's Republic of China*, University of California Press, 1977.

P. Pinstrup-Andersen, *Agricultural Research and Technology in Economic Development*, Longman, 1982.

D. Pyle, 'From Pilot Project to Operational Program in India: the Problems of Transition' in M. Grindle (ed.), *Politics & Policy Implementation in the Third World*, Princeton University Press, 1980.

D. Pyle, 'From Project to Program: the Study of the Scaling-Up/ Implementation Process of a Community-Level, Integrated Health, Nutrition, Population Intervention in Maharashtra', Ph.D dissertation, MIT, 1981.

N. S. Ramaswamy, 'Modernizing the Bullock-Cart: a Case of Appropriate Technology for India' in UNIDO, *Appropriate Industrial Technology for Low-Cost Transport for Rural Areas*, Monographs on Appropriate Industrial Technology, no. 2, UNIDO, 1979.

N. S. Ramaswamy, 'Draft Report on Draught Animal Power as a Source of Renewable Energy', FAO, Rome, Jan, 1981.

E. Rogers, *The Diffusion of Innovations*, Free Press, 1962.

E. Rogers, *The Diffusion of Innovations*, 3rd edn, Free Press, 1983.

D. Rondinelli, *Development Projects as Policy Experiments*, Methuen, 1983.

N. Rosenberg, 'On Technology Blending', ILO, World Employment Programme, Working Paper, no. 159, 1986.

W. Rybczynski *et al.*, *Appropriate Technology for Water Supply and Sanitation*, World Bank, 1982.

R. L. Sansom, 'The Motor Pump: a Case Study of Innovation and Development', *Oxford Economic Papers*, vol. 21(1), Mar. 1969.

E. Schuh and H. Tollini, 'Costs and Benefits of Agricultural Research', World Bank Staff Working Paper, no. 360, 1979.

E. F. Schumacher, *Small Is Beautiful*, Blond and Briggs, 1973.

G. Scobie, 'Investment in International Agricultural Research', World Bank Staff Working Paper, no. 361, 1979.

W. Shaner *et al.*, *Farming Systems Research: Guidelines for Developing Countries*, Westview, 1982.

A. Soedjarwo, 'Traditional Technology – Obstacle or Resource?: Bamboo–Cement Rain-Water Collectors and Cooking Stoves', The United Nations University, 1981.

R. Spence, 'Appropriate Technologies for Small-Scale Production of Cement and Cementitious Materials', UNIDO Forum on Appropriate Industrial Technology, New Delhi, 20–5 Nov. 1978.

F. Stewart, *Technology and Underdevelopment*, Macmillan, 1977.

F. Stewart, *Macro-Policies for Appropriate Technology*, Westview, 1987.

G. Sussman, 'The Pilot Project and the Choice of an Implementing Strategy: Community Development in India' in M. Grindle (ed.) *Politics and Policy*

Implementation in the Third World, Princeton University Press, 1980.

T. Tecle, 'The Evolution of Alternative Rural Development Strategies in Ethiopia: Implications for Employment and Income Distribution', Michigan State University, African Rural Employment Paper, no. 12, 1975.

UNIDO, *Agricultural Machinery and Rural Equipment in Africa: a New Approach to a Growing Crisis*, Sectoral Studies Branch, Division for Industrial Studies, Sectoral Studies Series no. 1, Mar. 1983.

S. Watanabe, (ed.), *Technology, Marketing and Industrialisation: Linkages Between Large and Small Enterprises*, Macmillan, 1983.

C. Weiss *et al.*, 'A Guide for the Program Manager: Methodologies for Measuring the Spread Effects of Aid Projects', An Appendix to Action Programs International's Final Report, Measuring the "Spread Effects" of AID Projects, US AID no. 930–0085, 1982.

W. Weiss *et al.*, 'The Design of Agricultural and Rural Development Projects' in D. Rondinelli (ed.), *Planning Development Projects*, Hutchinson & Ross, 1977.

C. Wong, 'Rural Industrialization in China' in R. Barker and R. Sinha (eds.), *The Chinese Agricultural Economy*, Westview, 1982.

G. Zeidenstein, 'The User Perspective: an Evolutionary Step in Contraceptive Service Programs', *Studies in Family Planning*, vol. 11(1), Jan. 1980.

Index